Pastoral Man in the Garden of Eden

Pastoral Man in the Garden of Eden

The Maasai of the Ngorongoro Conservation Area, Tanzania

BY KAJ ÅRHEM

Uppsala Research Reports in Cultural Anthropology
1985

Published by University of Uppsala, Department of Cultural Anthropology
in cooperation with The Scandinavian Institute of African Studies, Uppsala

The publication of this report has been financially
supported by Vilhelm Ekmans Universitetsfond

ISBN 91-7106-232-7
ISSN 0348-9507

Graphic design Jerk-Olof Werkmäster
Printed in Sweden by Almqvist & Wiksell Tryckeri, Uppsala 1985

Contents

PREFACE 9

ACKNOWLEDGEMENTS 10

1. INTRODUCTION 12

   Plan of the report 13

2. THE TANZANIAN MAASAI AND THE STATE 15

   The Maasai—"people of cattle" 15
   A historical outline 19
   The Masai Range Project 22
   Villagization 23
   Pastoralists, peasants and the state 26

3. THE HISTORY OF WILDLIFE CONSERVATION
   IN NGORONGORO 28

   The Ngorongoro Maasai 28
   The beginning of conservation rule 31
   The creation of the Ngorongoro Conservation Area 33
   The consolidation of conservation rule 35

4. PASTORAL RESOURCE USE IN NGORONGORO AND ITS
   ENVIRONMENTAL IMPACT 38

   The resource base 38
   Pastoral land use and settlement pattern 41
   Village, ward and zone 44
   People and livestock: Recent population trends 46
   *Population density, stocking rate and the carrying capacity
   of the land* 51
   The environmental impact 53
   Summary 56

5. LIVING CONDITIONS AMONG THE NGORONGORO
   MAASAI 64

   Housing and material possessions 64
   Livestock holdings 66

The problem of agriculture **68**
The food situation **71**
Trade and income: The ties to the market **75**
Resource development **82**
Health **86**
Education **90**
Summary **92**

6. CONFLICTING VIEWS ON DEVELOPMENT AND
CONSERVATION IN NGORONGORO **94**

The view of the pastoralists **95**
The view of the Conservation Authority **96**
A critical comment **97**

7. TOWARDS AND INTEGRATED APPROACH TO
DEVELOPMENT AND CONSERVATION **99**

Policy guidelines **102**
The wider context **109**

APPENDICES **111**

1. Seasonal Incidence of Principal Diseases: Monthly Treatment
Records from Endulen Hospital, 1980 **112**
2. Sex and Age Distribution of Principal Diseases: Treatment
Records from Endulen Hospital, 1980 **112**
3. School Attendance in the Ngorongoro Conservation Area,
1980 **113**
4. School Attendance in Relationship to Enrollment in the
Ngorongoro Conservation Area, 1980 **113**
5. Distribution of Basic Services in the Ngorongoro Conservation
Area **114**
6. Obstacles to Community Welfare: The View of the Pastoralists **115**

NOTES **116**

REFERENCES **120**

MAPS

1. Geographical Distribution of the Pastoral Maasai   16
2. Tanzanian Maasailand Today   21
3. The Serengeti-Ngorongoro Area: Seasonal Distribution of the Pastoral Population (before 1959)   30
4. The Ngorongoro Conservation Area   39
5. Pastoral Land Use and Settlement Pattern in the Ngorongoro Conservation Area   42
6. Distribution and Density of Domestic Stock and Plains Wildlife in the Ngorongoro Conservation Area, February 1980   55

FIGURES

1. Seasonal Variation in Rainfall in Different Parts of the Ngorongoro Conservation Area   40
2. Human and Livestock Population Trends in the Ngorongoro Conservation Area 1957–80   48
3. The Structure of the Pastoral Population in the Ngorongoro Conservation Area, 1978   49
4. Variations in Human and Livestock Population Densities in Different Pastoral Areas of East Africa   51
5. Food Consumption Profiles   73
6. Seasonal Incidence of Principal Diseases: Total Number of Cases of Treatment per Month at Endulen Hospital, 1980   86
7. Relative Incidence of Principal Diseases: Percentage of Total Number of Cases of Treatment at Endulen Hospital, 1980   87
8. Age and Sex Distribution of Principal Diseases: Percentage of Total Number of Cases of Treatment at Endulen Hospital, 1980   88
9. School Attendance in the Ngorongoro Conservation Area, 1980: Sex Distribution from Standard 1–7   91

PLATES

1. Boy (olayoni) with herd   58
2. Young man (olmorani) with herd   58
3. Permanent settlement (enkang)   59
4. Outside the house   59
5. Milking in the morning   60
6. Watering cattle at the hot spring in Esere   61
7. Family on the move along the Oldogom River (dry season, 1984)   61

8. Lion feeding on his kill—a zebra **62**
9. Wildebeest in the Ngorongoro Crater **62**
10. Kakesio village **63**
11. Women fetching water from the communal tap in Olbalbal village **63**

TABLES

1. Mean annual rainfall in different parts of the Ngorongoro Conservation Area **41**
2. Human and livestock population trends in the Ngorongoro Conservation Area, 1957–80 **47**
3. Changes in herd composition and livestock per capita ratios in Ngorongoro 1960–1980 **50**
4. Human and livestock population densities in the Ngorongoro Conservation Area, 1960–1980 **50**
5. Actual stocking rate in relation to estimated carrying capacity in different parts of the Ngorongoro Conservation Area, 1980 **53**
6. Plains ungulates in the Serengeti ecosystem: Population trends 1961–78 **56**
7. The importance of agriculture in the Ngorongoro Conservation Area before its prohibition 1975 **69**
8. Food consumption profiles: Dry season nutritional values per 100 g food **73**
9. Availability of consumer goods in the Ngorongoro Conservation Area: A sample of shops in different villages, September 1980 **76**
10. Cattle sale in the Ngorongoro Conservation Area 1961–80: Official marketing figures **78**
11. Barter terms of trade in the Ngorongoro Conservation Area, 1961–81 **80**
12. Income terms of trade in the Ngorongoro Conservation Area: Income from cattle sale 1961–80 **80**
13. Distribution of major water sources in the Ngorongoro Conservation Area (in use, August 1980) **83**
14. Distribution of livestock diseases in the Ngorongoro Conservation Area: The view of the pastoralists **85**
15. Distribution of diseases in the Ngorongoro Conservation Area: The view of the pastoralists **89**

Preface

And the Lord God planted a garden in Eden, in the east;
and there he put the man whom he had formed ...

(Genesis 2: 8)

The Biblical story about the garden of Eden—about how man in the
beginning lived in peace with every beast of the field and every bird in
the air—naturally comes to mind when visiting the Ngorongoro Conservation Area in Tanzania. Here, semi-normadic Maasai pastoralists
coexist with a remarkably rich variety of wildlife in a natural setting
of unspeakable beauty. One of the early travellers in Ngorongoro
recorded how he here witnessed "an unforgettably beautiful scene of
large herds of wildebeest, zebra and Grant's and Thomson's gazelles
grazing peacefully together with the cattle of the Maasai people
without showing any trace of shyness" (Merker, 1910: 175; own
translation). The same scene can still be seen today.

But, as in the Biblical story, the pastoral scene is transient. The
peaceful harmony conceals forces which threaten to shatter it. Man's
own strivings for betterment and the development and conservation
policies of the state tend to separate man and nature. Ambitious
development goals increasingly set man against nature, and the creation of National Parks and Game Reserves alienate indigenous people from their land by setting it apart—as islands of nature—for
international wildlife tourism. Thus, the Maasai of Serengeti in northern Tanzania were expelled from their homeland when Serengeti was
made a National Park towards the end of the colonial period. Today,
the Maasai of Ngorongoro are threatened by the same destiny.

This, in brief, indicates the central theme of this book: the articulation of development and conservation, the welfare of people and the
preservation of the environment, the economic interests of the state
and the needs of the local community. Let me add, finally, that the
book is offered as an interim report on current work. Many questions
are left unanswered and some of the material presented is incomplete.
I have ventured to publish the book in its present form because it
addresses issues of urgent and vital concern, not only for the people
of Ngorongoro, but for pastoral peoples, policy makers and planners
in East Africa in general.

Acknowledgements

This book is dedicated to the people of Ngorongoro. It fulfills part of my promise to them: to inform people in and outside Tanzania about their situation, in the hope of influencing policies in a direction which better serves their interests, and which is more conducive to the realization of their aspirations.

I owe particular gratitude to the people in Ndjureta, Sendui and Ilmesigio. I stayed with them many times and worked with them for weeks on end. They were always helpful, hospitable and generous. I hope my work in some way will benefit them.

Saiguran ole Senet helped me throughout my work in Tanzania. A Maasai, born and bred in Ngorongoro, he accompanied me on all my field trips—in the beginning as an assistant and interpreter, but later more as a friend and colleague. He also helped me sort out my field material during many work sessions in Dar es Salaam and Arusha. Lazaro ole Parkipuny, also a Ngorongoro Maasai by birth, introduced me to his people and their society. Currently the Member of Parliament for the Ngorongoro District, he is deeply committed to the welfare of his people. He was also a team member of the project, within the framework of which the work for this report was done. During discussions in Dar es Salaam and Uppsala he has helped me to shape many of the ideas contained in this report. I am greatly indebted to both.

My gratitude also extends to the staff of the Ngorongoro Conservation Area Authority, particularly to Joseph ole Kuwai, Sebastian Chuwa and Ndugu Mchanga. Though they may not agree with my conclusions, they were always friendly and helpful during my many stays in Ngorongoro.

The work on which this report is based was carried out while I held a position as a Research Fellow at the Bureau of Resource Assessment and Land Use Planning (now the Institute of Resource Assessment) at the University of Dar es Salaam. I want to thank my colleagues at the Bureau and its director, Adolfo Mascarenhas, for making my work possible and rewarding, both in a personal and a professional way.

While writing this report I have benefitted from the encouragement and critical comments of several people. I want particularly to mention Enid Nelson, Per Brandström, Michael Ståhl, Anders Hjort and Juhani Koponen. Though I have stubbornly insisted on the last word, they have all contributed to the report in one way or another.

10

The report was completed while I was working for the Research Programme on African Cultures at the Department of Cultural Anthropology, University of Uppsala. I am greatly indebted to the team leader of the Programme, Professor Anita Jacobson-Widding, for her encouragement and kind assistance in turning my draft into a publication.

Finally, I want to thank my wife and family who have been helpful in their own special way. As usual my wife has drawn most of the figures and maps.

Uppsala,
December 1984

1. Introduction

The Ngorongoro Conservation Area in northern Tanzania enjoys world renown for its scenic beauty and its abundant wildlife. In 1980 it was listed by UNESCO as a World Heritage Site in recognition of its outstanding international value as a natural and cultural legacy.[1] Extending over some 8 000 square km to the east of the Serengeti National Park, it includes the easternmost part of the vast Serengeti plains and the whole of the Ngorongoro highlands. In the centre lie the Ngorongoro Crater, with its spectacular concentration of wildlife, and the Olduvai Gorge, famed for its fossil remains of early man.

Ngorongoro is also the home of some 15 000 pastoral Maasai. Though much is known and written about the fauna and flora of the area and its prehistoric human and hominoid inhabitants, little is known about its present pastoral inhabitants, the Ngorongoro Maasai. This report seeks to redress this situation by providing factual information on the Ngorongoro Maasai and their system of resource use. Specifically, it aims to describe the socioeconomic conditions under which they live and to assess the environmental impact of their system of resource use.

This task is particularly important at the present time when the management policy and status of Ngorongoro as a Conservation Area is under reconsideration. In 1980 the Ngorongoro Conservation Area Authority called in an interdisciplinary team of researchers in the social and natural sciences under the coordination of the Bureau of Resource Assessment and Land Use Planning (BRALUP) at the University of Dar es Salaam to review the current policy and draft a new management and development plan for the area. The plan was completed in 1982. The present report is one result of the research work leading up to the plan.[2]

Apart from summarizing material presented in earlier reports and papers (often difficult of access; see list of references), this report essentially presents new and previously unpublished material. The field research, on which the report is based, was carried out between 1980 and 1982, when the author was a research fellow at BRALUP. During seven weeks in August and September 1980 a preliminary village survey was carried out, covering all villages in the Ngorongoro Conservation Area. The data was collected during village meetings and interviews with village leaders. Visits to schools, dispensaries and veterinary centres provided additional information. Unpublished census material on human and livestock populations was consulted at the Ngorongoro Conservation Area Authority headquarters. The survey yielded an overall picture of land use and settlement patterns, population trends and stocking rates, living conditions and community services in Ngorongoro.

The village survey was followed up with a more detailed study of the food situation among the Ngorongoro Maasai. This study was carried out in three localities of the Conservation Area—one in the eastern highlands, another on the western slopes of the central highlands, and the third on the dry northern plains—during the dry season (July–August) 1981, and the early wet season (March–April) 1982. Along with qualitative and quantitative data on household food intake, information was collected on grazing patterns and seasonal migrations, livestock holdings and herd structure, offtake and income from livestock sales. The study also included a survey of village shops (1981) in order to obtain a picture of the food supply situation of the pastoral community in Ngorongoro as a whole. Another follow-up visit to Ngorongoro was made in the summer (June–July) 1984. Only a few preliminary results of this last visit have been incorporated as notes in the present report.

The issues dealt with in the report have a direct bearing on the two major policy concerns of the Ngorongoro Conservation Area Authority: environmental conservation and community development. The articulation of conservation and development interests is, however, an area of general concern in East Africa and elsewhere in the Third World. The facts presented and the conclusions arrived at in the report may therefore be of interest outside the specific Tanzanian context.

Current conservation policies in East Africa tend to assume that pastoral land use and resource conservation are incompatible. Yet it is now an accepted truth among ecologists and range scientists that the East African savanna with its teeming wildlife is to a great extent created by pastoral man and his domestic stock in interaction with wild grazing ungulates (cf. Bell, 1971; Jacobs, 1975). Put briefly, the results of the present work suggest an alternative to current conservation policies in which conservation concerns and the subsistence interests of the pastoralists may be integrated into a comprehensive and environmentally sound development strategy.

PLAN OF THE REPORT

The report begins by placing the Maasai in the context of the Tanzanian state. National development policies and their consequences for the pastoral Maasai are sketched as a background to the more detailed examination of the history of conservation rule in Ngorongoro presented in Chapter Three. Chapter Four provides an outline of the system of pastoral land use in Ngorongoro, its resource base and environmental impact. Chapters Five and Six deal with the material living conditions of the Ngorongoro Maasai and their own perceptions of their social and economic reality. In the final chapter the findings of the report are summarized. The conclusions lead on to a series of policy recommendations, which are presented and briefly discussed in the context of current international conservation and development thinking at the end of the report.

2. The Tanzanian Maasai and the State

Tanzania is one of the wealthiest nations in Africa in terms of live-stock. According to the most recent livestock census (1978) there are some 12 million head of cattle in Tanzania.[3] Most of the domestic animals are kept by sedentary agro-pastoralists and mixed farmers in the tse-tse free areas of northern and central Tanzania. The largest herds and the highest stocking densities are found in higher-rainfall areas where crop production is the mainstay of the economy but where livestock, particularly cattle, play an important social and economic role. It has been estimated that about one quarter of the national cattle herd in Tanzania is kept by the agro-pastoral Sukuma on the margins of cultivated land in the Shinyanga, Mwanza and Tabora regions (cf. Brandström, Hultin and Lindström, 1979: 27). In the drier areas, occupied predominantly by semi-nomadic pastoral-ists, herds are more scattered and mobile, and stocking densities lower. Perhaps a tenth or less of the national cattle herd is kept by the pure pastoralists (Raikes, 1981: 147–56).

The major pastoral groups of Tanzania are the Maa-speaking Maasai and Baraguyu, and the Tatog-speaking Barabaig. Until recently they were all purely pastoral groups in the sense that agriculture played no or only a minimal role in subsistence. Over the past decade, however, increasing numbers of pastoralists, particularly Barabaig and Baraguyu, have, in response to pressures from the outside and the reduction of their resource base, taken to subsistence agriculture as a supplementary line of production, thus turning into agro-pastoral-ists (cf. Kjaerby, 1979).

The Maasai are by far the largest of the pastoral groups in Tanzania. Today the Tanzanian Maasai, thinly spread over northern Tanzania, number some 80–90 000 of the 250 000 or so pastoral Maasai living in the Rift Valley region of Kenya and Tanzania (Map 1).[4]

THE MAASAI—"PEOPLE OF CATTLE"

Maasai social and economic life centres around livestock. Cattle, sheep and goats form the basis of their subsistence. Milk, meat and blood are their dietary ideals, but in reality agricultural foods fre-quently supplement their pastoral diet, particularly during droughts and at the height of the dry season. Exchange of livestock for grain has probably always taken place between the pastoral Maasai and

15

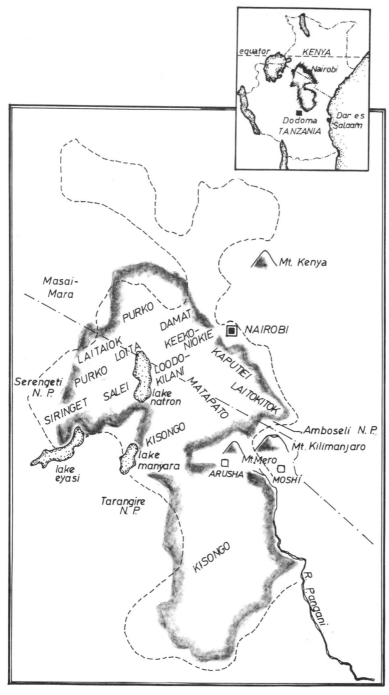

GREATEST EXTENSION OF THE
PASTORAL MAASAI

Based on Jacobs, 1965:117

PRESENT EXTENSION
MAASAILAND

Map 1. Geographical distribution of the pastoral Maasai.

their agricultural neighbours (Berntsen, 1970). Today grain, mainly in the form of maize flour, is a dry season staple along with milk. Though their pastoral economy is basically subsistence-oriented and the purely pastoral diet still highly valued, the need for grain firmly ties the Maasai to the economy of the larger society.

The herds of cattle kept by the pastoral Maasai are low-producing but sturdy and disease resistant. They serve as a store of food and insurance against disaster in an environment where drought is recurrent and livestock diseases endemic. Human population densities are low but animal-man ratios relatively high. Land use is transhumant, which means that grazing areas are seasonally kept fallow to allow for grass generation and to reduce grazing pressure. Rich grazing land is typically used during the dry season and left to recover during the wet, when people and livestock move to lower-potential areas.

Livestock means far more than food and economic security to the Maasai. Cattle in particular constitute a key value in Maasai culture. The entire social system is geared to cattle herding and moulded around the transhumant mode of subsistence. Cattle are a multiple purpose resource. The live produce and the different parts of the carcass are used as food, medicine, utensils, clothing and adornment. But cattle also signify wealth and confer status. They serve as a medium of exchange, legitimize marriage and symbolize social relationships. Cattle are objects of affection and of supreme religious significance. To the Maasai, then, cattle give meaning to life; they mean life itself.

Rights to livestock are at once individual and social. Livestock is handed down from father to son as legal property but may be kept in trust by a man's wives. Clan mates and stock friends also have claims on the family herd. Control over livestock is stratified; it implies a nesting set of vested interests involving individuals and groups both outside and within the immediate family, uniting as well as dividing the social sphere.

Land, too, is invested with cultural value and social meaning. The produce of the land, the green grass is a key symbol in Maasai ritual. Land is not owned by any one man but in a sense belongs to all. The Maasai are divided into territorial sections (iloshon) within which the members have priority rights in grazing. The largest sections are the Kisongo in Tanzania and the Purko in Kenya (Map 1). The section is subdivided into localities (inkutot) and neighbourhood clusters of settlements which effectively control customary grazing areas within the section territory. This hierarchy of rights in, and effective control over, grazing land is directly related to the requirements of herding in the semi-arid savanna environment: at times people and herds must be able to move over large areas in search of water and grass.

The Maasai social and political system bear out the pastoral adaptation. Social organization is flexible, allowing for periodic contraction, expansion and reorganization of herding units and social groups in response to changes in environmental conditions. Social groups are recruited on the basis of practical considerations of resource utilization and congeniality in cooperation rather than normative exigencies of kinship and residence rules. In an ecological perspective, Maasai society is designed to strike a viable balance between man, livestock and the physical environment—water and pastures.

Like the social system, the traditional political system is flexible and pragmatic. There are no ascribed or hereditary leaders. Authority rests with age set leaders, elected on the grounds of their moral conduct and personal qualities. Hierarchy and equality are coexistent political principles in Maasai society. Within age-groups equality is emphasized. The young men (ilmuran) form locality-based fellowships stressing sharing and communalism. Egalitarian solidarity and generosity are supreme values. Ilmuran are not allowed to eat alone. They cannot drink milk from their own family herds and always go around in groups. Influence, however, grows with seniority, increased knowledge and wisdom. As men grow older, wealth as an indicator of herding skills, comes to play an increasingly important role. Thus, elders control the younger age-groups, and community wide authority rests with the elders. The council of elders (enkigwana) is the principal decision-making body of the locality.

This summary presentation of Maasai culture points to the environmental rationality of the traditional pastoral system of land use, and stresses the emotional commitment to herding and cattle among the Maasai pastoralists. This is not to be confused with the notion of the "cattle complex" as originally presented by Herskovitz (1926) but demonstrates that what is economically necessary among the Maasai is emotionally charged and symbolically invested. The Maasai see themselves as herdsmen by tradition and sacred mandate. They are "people of cattle" (iltung'ana loo ngishu). As such they are, in their own view, distinct from the agriculturalists and hunters who surround them. Hunters, people without cattle, are seen as poor men. For the Maasai meat is not daily food; beef is, above all, sacred food. Agriculture is conceived of as desecration of the land on which cattle feed. Grass is food for cattle and therefore in a sense sacred too. The quintessential herdsman is the "big man" (olkitok), who builds up social influence by means of generosity and generalized exchange of his livestock, rather than the "rich man" (olkarsis), who accumulates wealth by reducing livestock exchanges (Galaty, 1981). The herdsman works for his family, his kin and his local community. Production is geared to the needs of the household. Beyond the household, food and property circulate within and between settlements along channels defined by kinship, friendship and age-group affiliation. This is, to the Maasai, the meaning of the "good life", the particular Maasai way of life.

At present the Tanzanian Maasai have increasing difficulties in reaching their own standards of good living. They are drawn into the mainstream of the national economy and the political machinery of the state. They are becoming increasingly dependent on economic and political forces beyond their control and hence less self-reliant. Their economic security and capacity to determine their own lives are reduced and their very existence as an ethnic group is threatened. Paradoxically, this situation has to a large extent been created by national development efforts ostensibly aimed at improving the well-being and living conditions of the rural peoples of Tanzania.

A HISTORICAL OUTLINE

In pre-colonial times, the Maasai controlled a vast area of land in Kenya and Tanzania. At the height of their power in the mid 19th century, Maasailand extended from central Kenya down to Ugogo and Uhehe in central Tanzania. Today they occupy less than two-thirds of their former territory. The great rinderpest, which hit East Africa in the 1890s, all but obliterated their herds.[5] Weakened by disease and the famine, which followed in its wake, the Maasai saw their best grazing land being taken over by white settlers and encroaching cultivators. The colonial land policies in Kenya and Tanganyika at the time favoured settler agriculture and indigenous small-holder farming.

In Kenya the "Maasai moves" of 1904 and 1911 excluded the Maasai from their dry season pastures and drought reserves in the highlands, which became known as the "white highlands". They were reserved for white settlement, while the Maasai were confined to the government controlled "Southern Reserve". In Tanganyika the Germans similarly attempted to confine the Maasai in a reserve on the arid Masai-steppe south of the Arusha-Moshi road, thus reserving the better lands of the northern half of the Tanganyikan Maasailand for white settlers. The attempt was unsuccessful; the white settler community in Tanganyika was not large enough, nor the German administration strong enough to enforce the plan (Huntingford, 1953; Parkipuny, 1983).

Yet agricultural encroachment and piecemeal land alienation for agricultural development took on considerable proportions in Tanganyikan Maasailand during the German rule. The Tanganyikan Maasai soon lost the rich land around Mt. Kilimanjaro and Mt. Meru to white settlers and indigenous farmers.

After the German defeat in the First World War, Tanganyika became a Mandated Territory administered by Britain. With the British came a period of relative peace and prosperity among the Tanganyikan Maasai. The Masai District covering most of Tanganyikan Maasailand was created in 1926 to impose order, and ostensibly to defend Maasai interests by controlling agricultural encroachment and livestock movements. On the whole, it seems that agricultural encroachment onto pastoral lands was, in fact, kept at bay by the benevolent British administration well into the 1930s (Parkipuny, 1975). Then, increasing demands on the colonial economy forced the British to tighten their grip on the traditional livestock economies. The "new colonialism" of the late inter-war period began to be felt even by the pastoralists. High productivity and bigger returns from the land became the slogans of the time (Iliffe, 1979).

Beginning in the late 1930s and continuing through the 1940s and 1950s a series of large scale land alienations took place in the centre of Tanganyikan Maasailand.[6] The Mbulu-Mbulu area, then inhabited by Maasai pastoralists, was settled for wheat production. Parts of the Ardai plains east of Arusha were virtually ruined by a heavily mechanised war-time wheat scheme. Monduli Juu and Makuyuni were largely taken over by European settlers and indigenous farmers. In Manyara several hundred thousand acres were appropriated by one European rancher. In 1947 the Maasai were evicted from the Sanya corridor. The following year Ol Molog, a dry season grazing area and ritual site of great importance to the Kisongo Maasai, was transferred to 15 European wheat farmers. In the early 1950s large tracts of land in Lolioro and Lepurko Essimingor were parcelled out to settlers for wheat and maize production. In the late 1950s, the borders of the Masai District, originally set out to secure Maasai rights in grazing-land, were changed to allow the rapidly growing numbers of WaArusha cultivators to take over pastoral lands in the Kisongo and Longido areas (Map 2).

In order to compensate the Maasai for the heavy losses of land, and to remedy some of the disastrous effects of the new land policies, the Masai Development Plan was launched in 1950. The aim of the programme was to modernize the traditional pastoral economy by providing improved services—pipelines, dams and boreholes—and by combating the tse-tse. The programme collapsed in 1955. Its most lasting effect was a notable resource depletion. In the years that followed, colonial development efforts in Maasailand were devoted to redress the damages done by past undertakings (Parkipuny, 1975).

The general thrust of the colonial land policy—that of taking over

20

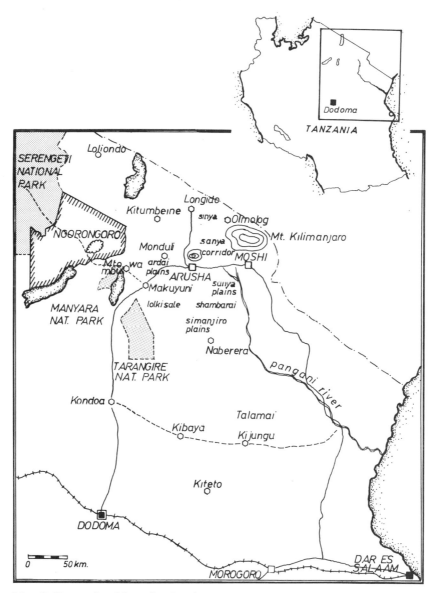

Map 2. Tanzanian Maasailand today.

pastoral lands and putting them to more intensive use while compensating the pastoralists with largely ineffective extension services —continued after Independence in 1961 and even up to the present day. Large tracts of land on the Ardai plains and in the Lenkijabe hills near Monduli were taken over in the 1970s for military installations and a national wheat scheme. Massive encroachments by agriculturalists have continued into the Sinya plains, the Monduli mountain, the

21

Loliondo highlands and the Kijungu-Kibaya area of southern Maasailand. In the north, cultivation now extends far beyond Monduli and deep into the Simanjiro and Shambarai areas. In 1980 an area of 1 500 square km in Lolkisale, east of Tarangire National Park, was leased to a private multinational agrobusiness company. Currently, there are advanced plans for setting up large scale, state-owned wheat and barley farms in the Loliondo area.

THE MASAI RANGE PROJECT

The obvious effect of this situation has been an increased subsistence stress among the pastoralists and heavier pressure on the dwindling pastoral resources. The Maasai and other pastoral groups in Tanzania have been pushed out onto marginal lands, often being forced to use on a year-round basis grazing areas which they previously used only for wet season grazing. Poverty and a widening gap between prosperous and poor pastoralists have turned many pastoralists into agro-pastoralists and urban squatters. Competition for land between pastoralists and cultivators has hardened. The Range Management Act of 1964 was in part a response to these processes. It aimed at regulating land use in areas where the interests of livestock production and agriculture were in conflict. The Masai Range Commission was set up in the same year to administer the Act and register ranching associations in Maasailand. It was later instrumental in the launching of the USAID-financed Masai Range and Management Project in 1970. The project was the most ambitious and costly ever launched in Tanzanian Maasailand. By establishing ranching associations and an efficient marketing system it sought to achieve "a sustained high level of livestock offtake in the Masai District, consistent with proper range management and Tanzanian development goals" (Hoben, 1976). The objective was to be achieved, on the one hand, by means of developing the livestock-related infrastructure through range management plans, disease control, water development, market improvements and the introduction of improved bulls and, on the other, by creating ranching associations to secure rights of occupancy and to manage the infrastructure.[7]

The project initially met with a positive response from the Maasai. They were promised dips, water supplies and drugs for their livestock. People were willing to form ranching associations. Indeed the concept of "range" gained a symbolic value and in parts of Maasailand the newest age group was given the name *range* (Parkipuny, 1979: 145). The area chosen for the initial attention of the project, Talamai, attracted large numbers of people and stock. High stocking levels resulted. Land deteriorated, bush encroached and water was soon inadequate to meet the inflated demands.

In other parts of the project area, the opposite situation arose. The promised facilities never materialized and people lost interest. The project was not able to provide the planned services, and more serious still, could not secure rights of occupancy in any of the associations formed. In 1975 there were eight ranching associations in some stage of formation. When the project ended five years later, in 1980, they were all dissolved. The reason was basically a conflict between the project goals and the priorities of the national development policies at the time. The associations had lost their cattle marketing functions to the Tanzania Livestock Marketing Corporation (TLMC) in 1974. The legal status of the associations was seriously undermined by the villagization programme launched in 1973–74 (described below). The Masai Range Commission, which had been instrumental in initiating the whole project, had ceased to function already in 1972, when it was absorbed by the new regional administration following upon the decentralization reform the same year.

On the technical side, the project had achieved a great deal, but without a supporting institutional framework to manage the technical inputs the positive effects were partly lost. Dips and water points were left unattended and fell into disrepair. Socially and economically the project was a failure. It failed to establish a monitoring system for range conditions and stocking levels. Sales of livestock did not increase, while overstocking and range deterioration in some parts of the project area reached alarming proportions. Finally, the project failed to reward local initiatives in fund-raising and organization, to involve the Maasai in planning and implementation, and, above all, to secure their legal rights of occupancy.

VILLAGIZATION

In 1973 the Tanzanian government launched the nationwide villagization programme. All rural Tanzanians were required to move into nucleated villages, called development villages. After the initial difficulties in implementing the villagization programme in different parts of the country the government realized that development among pastoralists had to take a different course from among settled agriculturalists. Up to 1974, rural development in Tanzania had basically meant agricultural modernization. Livestock development among traditional livestock producers had meant sedentarization and a change from extensive pastoralism to mixed farming—intensified and modernized livestock production in combination with crop cultivation. This is, by and large, still the view of policy makers and state bureaucrats, but after 1974 it was officially recognized that villagization and development in pastoral areas had to be adapted to pastoral conditions. The concept of "livestock development villages"—as distinguished from agricultural development villages—was created and obtained official acceptance (Parkipuny, 1979: 154).

Livestock development villages are defined as those villages where livestock production is the main economic activity. The model type of the livestock development village was to comprise a central settlement area and a village range, divided into a core area for the milk herd and an outlying range for dry- and wet season use by the main beef-herd. The basic settlement units, the kraal camps, were to be arranged in a circular or semi-circular layout with the village services in the centre (Hoben, 1976; Parkipuny, 1979).

In 1974–75 the villagization programme was launched in Maasailand under the name of Operation Imparnati (*imparnati* means "permanent habitations") with the purpose of settling the pastoral Maasai in livestock development villages. Planning and implementation teams were sent out from the district headquarters to inform the pastoralists about the operation and eventually to induce them to move into villages. The pastoralists were told to choose a site for the new village settlement and to move there within a period fixed by the district officials, usually two months. To judge from the available records, the operation was generally carried out rather smoothly. According to one official "the pastoralists were easier to deal with than the cultivators" (quoted in Ndagala, 1982: 30). The village layouts were generally flexibly imposed and adapted to local conditions. Existing land use and settlement patterns were usually accepted as the ground plan for resettlement. As a result, movement tended to be relatively minor and seldom covered distances of more than five km. The actual relocation of boma sites did not have major social and economic effects.[8]

On the other hand the campaign was poorly planned. It was, as one commentator put it (Parkipuny, 1979: 54), a mere "lumping together" of bomas around already existing trading centres. There was no popular mobilization for specific purposes. It was precisely an "operation", a campaign imposed upon the pastoralists. In some instances the level of persuasion was, in fact, very crude and coercion did occur. In at least two cases, both in the Ngorongoro district, the implementation teams burned settlements to force the pastoralists to move to new sites (Parkipuny, 1979: 155; own survey 1981–82).

By mid 1975 more than 2 000 Maasai were reported to have moved into development villages (Parkipuny, 1979: 154). By May 1976 an estimated 36% of the total population in Kiteto district and 31% in Monduli district had been resettled in 27 out of a planned 139 agricultural and livestock development villages (Hoben, 1976: 56).

The Maasai reacted to the villagization programme as they had reacted to government interventions in the recent past: with apparent indifference and without resistance. They accepted it as a new force in their reality, much as they responded to environmental changes in general. The Maasai faced the obligation to form villages with mixed feelings of hope and distress.[9] Some saw in the campaign an opportunity: they hoped that the new policy would give them secure rights of occupancy in their land, much as they had hoped some years earlier when agreeing to join the ranching associations of the Masai Range Project. They thought that it might help them defend their pastures and water sources against agricultural encroachment. Possibly they also expected from the policy greater autonomy and economic security. The initial reaction of compliance was, at least in part, a tactical and strategic response to achieve these ends.

But there was at the same time a widespread worry among the Maasai about the villagization programme. They saw in villagization another step taken by the government to subjugate them and conquer their land. They feared that they would have to give up their traditional clothing and housing, that they would be forced to destock and have their herds collectivized, and that they would be compelled to become "wajamaa" which they believed meant sharing everything, including wives and children (Ndagala, 1982: 29).

Villagization imposed a new authority structure on the traditional community and represented a step towards the imposition of a new settlement and land use pattern, difficult to reconcile with the pastoral values. The new hierarchy of political offices—the village chairman, secretary and manager—weakened the traditional leadership. It placed the centre of authority outside the local community. The move towards a more nucleated and sedentary settlement pattern was experienced by many pastoralists as a threat to the transhumant way of life and the resource base on which their society rested. Similarly, the stipulated restrictions on herd and settlement size touched the very core of the Maasai culture: livestock as a multiple resource and societal value. Restrictions on individual livestock holdings meant to the Maasai an infringement on their freedom and a reduction of their capacity to subsist. At the same time the Maasai also saw in the villagization programme a possibility of increasing their control over pastures, a possibility at least ostensibly reinforced by the latest national livestock policy (Ministry of Livestock Development, 1983). The hopes and fears expressed by the Maasai in response to the villagization campaign all reflected their most basic concerns: economic security and political autonomy.

In a national, political and economic perspective, there are good reasons for the Tanzanian Maasai to be sceptical about current development policies and concerned about their future as an ethnic group. The villagization campaign and the Masai Range Project both form part of a more comprehensive strategy of societal transformation working against the pastoralists.

Since Independence in 1961 Tanzania has aspired to a socialist politicial and economic development. The Arusha Declaration in 1967 firmly committed the nation to a policy of socialism and self-reliance. The policy signalled a break with the colonial past and the emergence of a truly nationalistic ideology. Development was defined as development towards democracy, equality between people, political autonomy and economic self-reliance. Rural development policies were consequently radicalized in accordance with the basic goals of the Arusha Declaration. The ujamaa policy, based on the creation of ujamaa villages where people were to live and work together on communally owned land, became the blue-print for rural development.[10] But the policy failed in its two most crucial respects; it failed to mobilize the peasants for its political goals, and it failed to induce the peasants to produce the agricultural surplus necessary for achieving the ambitious economic development goals.[11]

As a consequence, the state tightened its grip on the peasants. While the ujamaa policy had sought a radical socialist transformation of rural society based on the voluntary creation of ujamaa villages, the villagization programme in the mid 1970s became compulsory. It was ostensibly meant to bring basic social services to the peasants, but in effect implied greater government control. The move towards greater political control over the peasantry was reflected in the economic policies during the latter half of the 1970s. The state concentrated its investments to large-scale and export-oriented agro-industries. More than half of the rural development budget for the period 1977–79 went to the development of state-controlled plantations, farms and ranches (Ståhl, 1980: 83).

The same general trends are discernible in the evolution of livestock policies.[12] State involvement in the livestock sector has grown steadily since Independence. Livestock development has come to mean the creation and expansion of large scale, state-owned beef ranches and dairy farms. The third five-year plan (1976–81) allocated some 41% of its total livestock development budget to beef ranching alone. All in all, industrial beef- and dairy-production units together accounted for about 80% of the total livestock development budget (Raikes, 1981: 161). The impressive expansion of the ranch sector has, however, yielded poor results. It has neither produced the meat needed for the urban market, nor the profits expected. And it has taken place at the expense of the pastoral and agro-pastoral peasantry. The development of state-controlled beef ranches and dairy farms has steadily and increasingly channeled resources away from the pastoral producers.

The history of the pastoral peoples of Tanzania since the turn of the century is a history of land loss and marginalization. Grazing land has been taken over by individual farmers, private companies and the state, usually in that order. Development projects have been investment-oriented, aiming at the rationalization and industrialization of the livestock economy rather than the development of the pastoral communities. Current state policies tend—intentionally or unintentionally—to eliminate pastoral forms of land use rather than improve them. The concentration of people in villages has led not only to an increased pressure on range lands, but also to an intensified competition between pastoralists and agriculturalists, and a growing dependence among pastoralists on agricultural foods. In many villages the concentration of social services has attracted agriculturalists and marginalized pastoralists. There are cases of whole villages created for the pastoralists which have been entirely taken over by cultivators and agro-pastoralists (Kjaerby, 1979, 1980; see also Ndagala, 1982). The commercialization of livestock production has tended to increase resource competition and economic differentiation among the pastoralists themselves. The gap between rich and poor herders has widened. For the most part the Ngorongoro Maasai have been spared the worst consequences of these processes, but some of them are visible also in Ngorongoro. This will be a topic of subsequent chapters.

3. The History of Wildlife Conservation in Ngorongoro

State intervention and land alienation for development purposes have taken many forms in Tanzanian Maasailand. As was shown in the previous Chapter, natural rangeland has given way to beef ranches, wheat schemes and smallholder farms. But there is another form of land alienation which has come to play an increasingly important role in the national development strategies of Kenya and Tanzania over the past three decades, and which has had a profound impact on the pastoral societies in the region: the creation and expansion of wildlife reserves.

Since the 1950s a large number of game reserves and national parks have been established in Kenya and Tanzania. In East African legal terminology national parks and game reserves exclude by law all kinds of human habitation and subsistence activities (except those related to the tourist industry). Game controlled areas and conservation areas allow human habitation and certain forms of land use subject to strict controls. Maasailand is today filled with one or the other form of wildlife reserve. On the Kenyan side there are the Amboseli National Park and the Maasai Mara Reserve. On the Tanzanian side there are the Serengeti, Manyara, Tarangire, Arusha and Kilimanjaro National Parks and the Ngorongoro Conservation Area, all extending over traditional Maasai grazing land. In this Chapter I describe the development of wildlife conservation and its impact on the pastoral community in the Serengeti-Ngorongoro area.[13]

THE NGORONGORO MAASAI

The Serengeti plains and the Ngorongoro highlands have been inhabited by Maasai pastoralists since the 17th century and before that by various pastoral Tatog groups, ancestors of the present-day Barabaig. It was not until the 1830s, after subjugating and driving out the Tatog peoples, that the Maasai firmly gained control over the area. At the time of the disastrous rinderpest epidemics in the 1890s, the Siringet and Salei Maasai occupied the area. But the pest—and the smallpox and famine which followed in its wake—sent the whole of Maasailand into turmoil. The disaster hit differentially. The Ngorongoro highlands were less affected than the Serengeti plains. People from Serengeti and the lowlands north and east of Ngorongoro migrated into the highlands in search of pastures and food. Fighting erupted in several places. The Loita Maasai came down from the north on the weakened Siringet and drove them out of the Serengeti-Ngorongoro area. The situation remained static under German colonial rule. Meanwhile, the different Maasai groups regained their strength. When administrative controls were relaxed during the First World War, the Purko and Kisongo Maasai converged on the Loita and ousted them definitely from the Ngorongoro highlands. One of the final battles was fought in the Empakaai Crater in the eastern part of the Ngorongoro highlands where the Loita were thoroughly defeated. The Purko Maasai then returned to their homeland in Kenya and the Kisongo came to dominate the Ngorongoro highlands, while the Siringet and Salei Maasai reoccupied the Serengeti and Sale plains west and north of the highlands (Fosbrooke, 1962, 1972; cf. Maps 1 and 4).

Since the 1920s there has prevailed relative social stability in the Serengeti-Ngorongoro area. The number of pastoralists and the size of the domestic herds have fluctuated according to climatic variation and the incidence of livestock diseases. The human population has increased moderately but steadily, while the cattle population has oscillated around a fairly stable level. In 1929 the area held some 139 000 cattle and 227 000 sheep and goats (Masai-Monduli District Book, 1929). Twenty-five years later, in 1954, there were some 10–11 000 Maasai pastoralists with 122 000 cattle and 208 000 small stock in the area (Grant, 1957). The greater part of the pastoral population occupied what today constitutes the Ngorongoro Conservation Area, but some 1 000–1 200 of them, with 25 000 head of cattle and 15 000 goats and sheep, lived in the Western Serengeti, the present-day Serengeti National Park. They were settled around the permanent water sources at Moru, Sironet (Seronera), Bosigiya, Laibordoroto and Engare Nanyuki (see Map 3). The Western Serengeti was also used as a seasonal grazing area by a much larger population, including the Maasai living in the Oldoinyo Oogol hills and in the Kakcsio-Endulen area.

Currently (1980) some 14–15 000 Maasai inhabit the easternmost fringe of the Serengeti plains and the Ngorongoro highlands, keeping about 118 000 cattle and 145 000 small stock. Since 1959 the pastoralists are confined to the Ngorongoro Conservation Area. I refer to the Maasai living in this area as the Ngorongoro Maasai. They do not, however, form a sociologically bounded unit, but are composed of various sub-groupings of different Maasai sections, principally the Kisongo, Siringet and Salei Maasai. Nor is their present homeland ecologically bounded; the Ngorongoro Conservation Area is an area defined by administrative considerations and political circumstances

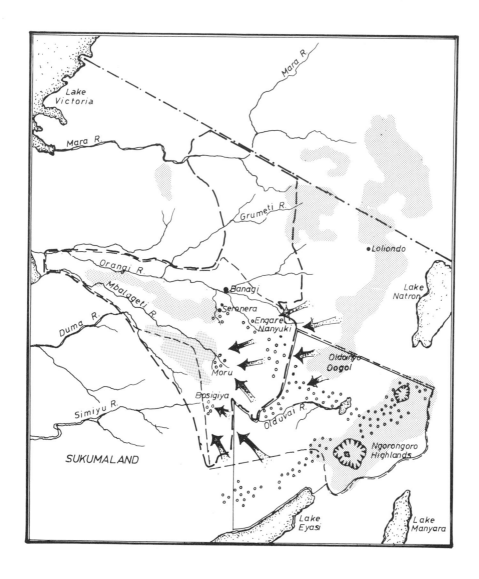

Hills and Highlands
Serengeti National Park, before 1959
Serengeti National Park, present extension
Ngorongoro Conservation Area
Regular Dry Season Maasai settlement areas before 1959
Regular Dry Season Movements

Map 3. The Serengeti-Ngorongoro area: Seasonal distribution of the pastoral population before 1959.

(described below). It borders on the Serengeti National Park in the west and extends to the Rift Valley Escarpment in the east. In the south it is bounded by the Highland Forest Reserve and the agricultural settlements of the Oldeani-Karatu area, while its northern boundary cuts through the rugged Oogol mountains.

The Serengeti-Ngorongoro environment is typical of Maasailand in general: a mixture of open, short grassland on the low-lying plains, hilly parkland and tall grasslands and forests in the highlands with mountain peaks rising to over 3 000 m. This combination of dry, hot lowlands and more humid, cool highlands has for centuries provided the setting for pastoral communities in East Africa. The pastoralists and their herds of livestock seasonally alternate between the two types of environment according to a transhumant pattern of land use, finely tuned to environmental resources and constraints. The highland pastures are grazed during the dry season and the plains used in the wet.

The cultural reality and the social system of which the Ngorongoro Maasai form a part embrace the whole of Maasailand on both sides of the Kenya-Tanzania border. Similarly, the pastoral ecosystem extends far beyond the boundaries of the Ngorongoro Conservation Area: people and livestock temporarily move north into the Loliondo hills, and east to the floor of the Rift Valley in search of water and pasture. Conversely, people and livestock from outside the area may also at times, particularly during periods of drought, move into the Ngorongoro highlands from the drier areas to the north and east.

THE BEGINNING OF CONSERVATION RULE

The Serengeti-Ngorongoro area has been recognized as a wildlife area since the turn of the century. A fragmented legislation to protect its wildlife was drafted by the German colonial administration, but it was never enacted. In 1907, two German settlers occupied the Ngorongoro Crater, but since their eviction during the First World War, hunting and wildlife conservation have become the dominant interests of the British colonial administration. The first comprehensive conservation legislation was the Game Preservation Ordinance introduced by the British in 1921. In 1928 the Ngorongoro Crater was declared a Closed Reserve. All hunting and agriculture in the reserve were forbidden by law. The remainder of the Serengeti-Ngorongoro area was declared a Closed Reserve in 1930. Yet, hunting for sport continued unabated in large parts of the reserve.

Towards the end of the 1930s hunting had assumed such proportions that the British administration became concerned about the future of the area as a wildlife preserve. Consequently in 1940 the area was declared a National Park under a new Game Ordinance of that same year. The boundaries of the Park were revised in 1948 under the National Park Ordinance, but it was not until 1951 that the legislation was actively enforced. The year 1951 thus marks the beginning of effective wildlife protection in the Serengeti-Ngorongoro area. The legislation did not yet affect the rights of the people residing in the Park; indeed they were explicitly protected. The resident Maasai were given positive assurances by the government that there would be no interference with their rights to live and subsist in the Park. However, in the course of the decade conservation measures became increasingly strict: hunting was forbidden, human settlement and movement of domestic stock subjected to multiple restrictions, the use of fire strictly regulated, and—in 1954—all cultivation prohibited in the Park. Not surprisingly, the local pastoralists and cultivators reacted strongly.

Both pastoralists and cultivators resented the reduction of their freedom and joined in outspoken criticism of the hardening conservation measures. Particularly, they reacted against the prohibition on agriculture. They managed to mobilize support from the district and provincial administration for their stand against the Park authorities. As a consequence of the conflict, and because of the strong interests involved, discussions were initiated at government level which led to the publication in 1956 of the White Paper (Sessional Paper No 1). This paper suggested a compromise solution to the conflict. It recommended the breaking-up of the Serengeti National Park into three smaller parks: the first, the Western Serengeti, consisting of the bush country west of the Serengeti plains; the second, consisting of the Ngorongoro Crater and the Northern Highland Forest Reserve, and the third, the Empakaai Crater. These three parks would be set aside exclusively for wildlife protection while the rest of the original Park would be opened up for cultivation and pastoral land use.

The proposal caused international concern and provoked a storm of protests from conservationists in Europe and North America. The same year, 1956, a Committee of Enquiry was appointed by the colonial government to study the issue and propose a new policy solution to the crisis. The American Wildlife Management Institute and the American Committee for International Wildlife Protection sent out a team of natural scientists, and the Fauna Preservation Society of London commissioned the late Prof. W. H. Pearsall to carry out a similar investigation. His report, issued after a two-month visit to the area, had a profound influence upon the course of events and, in effect, came to form the scientific basis for the final recommendations of the Committee of Enquiry, which were presented in Government Paper Number 5, 1958.

THE CREATION OF THE NGORONGORO
CONSERVATION AREA

The recommendations resulted in the partition of the original Serengeti National Park according to the Ngorongoro Conservation Ordinance Number 14 of 1959. As of July 1st, 1959 the Park was split into two separate units: the western part (formerly called Western Serengeti) retained the original name of the Park and was designated as an exclusive wildlife area, while the eastern part, including the eastern fringe of the Serengeti plains, the Kakesio-Endulen area (previously outside the Park) and the whole of the Ngorongoro highlands, came to form the Ngorongoro Conservation Area.

Although in the colonial records this solution appears as a compromise approved by the Maasai, the decision in effect compelled all the inhabitants of the Western Serengeti to abandon their homeland, their pastures and their water sources. Under pressure from international wildlife interests and the colonial administration, the Maasai agreed to leave the rich grazing areas in Serengeti and the permanent springs and streams of Sironet and Moru. Most of them moved into the Ngorongoro Conservation Area where they were promised permanent rights in the land as well as new water supplies in compensation for those that they had lost.

The Ngorongoro Conservation Area was created as an area of multiple land use; an area in which several different but compatible land use interests were to be combined within an integrated, comprehensive land use policy. These interests included—apart from the basic policy concern to conserve the national resources in the area—the subsistence interests of the resident pastoralists and cultivators, tourist interests and archaeological interests.

Initially the decision-making body administering the Conservation Area consisted of four expatriate officers and four Maasai elders representing the interests of the resident pastoralists, under the chairmanship of the colonial district officer. However, within a year the original organizational set-up of the administration was changed: it had failed to bridge the differences between the technical officers and the local pastoralists. A new Advisory Board appeared in 1961, now without Maasai representation. In fact, there was no Maasai representation in the successive conservation authorities until 1981, when the Member of Parliament for the Ngorongoro District—who happens to be a Maasai—was included in the Board of Directors of the Ngorongoro Conservation Area Authority.

The first management plan of the Ngorongoro Conservation Area was drawn up in 1960 by an administrative team. The plan was revised in 1961 by H. Fosbrooke, who took over as the Chairman of the Advisory Board. In 1963, the Advisory Board was disbanded, and a new division was set up in the Ministry of Lands, Forestry and Wildlife in the now independent Republic of Tanzania. The Unit was headed by a Conservator who was made directly responsible to the Minister. Fosbrooke was appointed the first Conservator that same year. In 1965 he was succeeded by Solomon ole Saibull, the first Tanzanian Conservator. A year later, in 1966, the Canadian ecologist H. J. Dirschl was commissioned to rewrite the existing plan. The result was a new plan with practical guidelines for implementing the policy of multiple land use. An important feature of the plan was the delineation of land use zones: zones for exclusive wildlife and forest protection, for agricultural and pastoral development, for tourism and for the protection of archaeological sites.

However, the 1966 plan was never given the official endorsement that was necessary to make it a blueprint for management and development in the Ngorongoro Conservation Area. Its implementation was overtaken by a series of political events which culminated in the so-called "conservation controversy" in 1968–69. The controversy emanated from escalating tensions between conservationist and economic interests in the Conservation Area. It concerned the use of the resources in the area in general and the question of agriculture in particular. It was in fact very much a parallel to the crisis in the late 1950s which led to the creation of the Serengeti National Park and the Ngorongoro Conservation Area.

Once again there was a polarization of interests between different political groups in the country. There were strong forces within the Ministry of Agriculture, now the parent Ministry of the Unit, to dissolve the Ngorongoro Conservation Area as an administrative unit; a bill was proposed to the effect that the greater part of the Conservation Area would lose conservation status and be turned over to the Masai Range Commission for livestock and agricultural development, while the remaining parts—the Ngorongoro and Empakaai Craters and the Forest Reserve—would obtain national park status (Cabinet Paper 6, 1969). The proposal was backed by the Minister of Agriculture, the Principal Secretary of the Ministry, the Regional Commissioner and the Member of Parliament for the district. In fact, the Minister had secured Presidential and Cabinet consent to propose the bill to the Parliament the same year (Cabinet Paper 1, 1969; cited in Parkipuny, 1981). However, the bill was strongly—and in the end successfully—opposed by the Conservator, the Director of Natural Resources in the Ministry and international conservation agencies.

When the controversy took the form of a heated public debate in national and international mass media, the President intervened and curtailed further debate. In 1970, the Ministry of Agriculture was reorganized. The Ngorongoro Conservation Unit now came under the responsibility of the new Ministry of Natural Resources and Tourism. The former Conservator moved to a new post as Director of National Parks. The Ngorongoro Conservation Area came out of the conflict with its original boundaries and official land use policy intact, but with a new leadership and a different institutional attachment.

The shift in institutional attachment, placing the Conservation Unit under the Ministry of Natural Resources and Tourism, marked a new trend in actual conservation management. The conservationist stance of the Unit hardened. By 1972, the political pendulum had swung over to the other extreme: strong conservationist forces within the Ministry of Natural Resources and Tourism, backed by powerful international wildlife interests, sought an amendment of the Ngorongoro Conservation Area Ordinance of 1959 which would have turned a large part of the Conservation Area into an exclusive wildlife area. But in the end compromise prevailed, and in 1975 a new Conservation Ordinance came into effect. The Ngorongoro Conservation Unit was renamed the Ngorongoro Conservation Area Authority (NCAA). The Ordinance included a clause stipulating that the NCAA should not only preserve and develop the natural resources of the area, but also safeguard and promote the interests of the Maasai citizens engaged in cattle ranching and dairy industry in the area. The Conservation Authority now became a parastatal institution with a Board of Directors and a Conservator to be appointed by the President.

THE CONSOLIDATION OF CONSERVATION RULE

After the eviction of the Maasai from the Western Serengeti serious efforts were made by the successive administrations of the Conservation Area to promote the interests of the resident pastoralists, particularly in the areas where the Siringet Maasai had settled—in Kakesio, Endulen and the Oldoinyo Oogol mountains. These efforts were mainly concerned with developing the range water supplies in compensation for the permanent, natural water sources lost in Western Serengeti at the creation of the Serengeti National Park. Thus, between 1959–1965, three boreholes and three dams were constructed in the areas mentioned. In 1981 all three boreholes were, however, out of order and had been so intermittently for many years. Similarly, all three dams were defunct. On the whole, the artificial water supplies constructed over the years in Ngorongoro have proved grossly inadequate (see Chapter Five below).

At the same time the pastoralists experienced a steady shrinkage of their grazing land. Several prime grazing grounds in the Conservation

Area have, since 1959, been closed to grazing and settlement. These include the Ngorongoro, Empakaai and Olmoti Craters, the Northern Highland Forest Reserve, the Lemakarot and Olósirwa mountain slopes, Olduvai Gorge and the Laitole archaeological site (Map 4). The shrinkage of the pastoral resource base has considerably reduced the pastoral carrying capacity of the Conservation Area. Though the restrictions tend to be flexibly implemented by the Conservation Authority—mainly due to limitations of personnel and financial resources—the fact that they exist has created much resentment among the pastoralists towards the Conservation Authority.

Perhaps the most critical land loss was experienced by the pastoralists living on the floor of the Ngorongoro Crater. As a consequence of the villagization programme of the mid 1970s and the hardening conservation rule they were evicted from the Ngorongoro Crater in the late 1970s. Grazing and watering of livestock in the Crater, covering an area of some 250 square km, were prohibited. Since the Maasai occupation of the Serengeti-Ngorongoro area, the Crater had been the home and dry season base of a small community of Maasai pastoralists, as well as an essential dry season grazing ground and salt lick for the pastoralists living in the surrounding highlands. This community, comprising at the time of eviction some three to four settlements, was now moved to a newly founded village on the western rim of the Crater.

The Ngorongoro Conservation Area Ordinance of 1975 prohibited all cultivation within the Conservation Area. Prior to this date, cultivation had been allowed as one form of land use under the multiple land use policy. Despite the pressures exerted by the Conservation Authority to restrict agriculture in Ngorongoro in the late 1960s and early 1970s, cultivation had reached considerable proportions by the mid 1970s. All over the Conservation Area small scale subsistence cultivation of maize and beans provided supplementary food to the pastoralists. This supplement to the pastoral diet was considered important by the pastoralists, particularly in the dry season. The availability of grain crops within the Conservation Area made the pastoralists less dependent upon the insecure market and the irregular supply of grain from outside. To the Ngorongoro Maasai, then, the prohibition on agriculture meant an infringement of their land rights and a blow to their vulnerable subsistence economy.

As in 1959, when the pastoralists were urged by the government to move out of Western Serengeti and abandon the pastures and water sources there, the authorities now promised compensation, this time for giving up agriculture. The pastoralists were promised sufficient supplies of grain and other commodities in the village shops, together with veterinary services and help in improving their livestock economy through dairying and ranching. The Regional Trading Corporation (RTC) was to take care of the supply and distribution of grain to the villages, and the Conservation Authority was to be put in charge of livestock development. As is documented in later chapters of this report, the promises have not been fulfilled. Grain and other essential consumer goods continue to be in short supply in the Conservation Area. No grain storage facilities or stocks against hard times have been established, and plans for improving the livestock economy are still, at best, in the draft stage.

4. Pastoral Resource Use in Ngorongoro and its Environmental Impact

Management and administration in Ngorongoro have, for the past decade, been characterized by a hardening conservation stance. This tendency reflects the view of the Conservation Authority that pastoralism and the modernization of the traditional livestock economy are incompatible with environmental conservation. The Conservation Authority holds that the pastoral population and the herds of domestic livestock in Ngorongoro are approaching and locally surpassing the carrying capacity of the land. The pastoralists are consequently seen as a threat to the wildlife and vegetation in the area. Yet, prior to the inter-disciplinary investigation on which this report is based, no in-depth study of population trends and the environmental impact of pastoralism in Ngorongoro had been carried out. As will be shown in this and the following chapters, a closer examination of available information gives a picture of the overall ecological situation in Ngorongoro very different from that painted by the Conservation Authority.

THE RESOURCE BASE

Two ecological regimes dominate in Ngorongoro: the semi-arid plains in the north and west, and the cooler and wetter highlands in the central and eastern parts of the area. The plains include parts of the vast Serengeti and Sale short-grass plains, separated by the rugged mountains and hills of Oldoinyo Oogol. The highland massif contains the peaks of the Olosirwa and Loolmalasin mountains, the extinct volcanoes Lemakarot and Satiman, and the calderas of Ngorongoro, Olmoti and Empakaai (see Map 4).

Rainfall is seasonal and varies with altitude. The year is divided into a long dry season from June to October and a wet season from November to May (Fig 1). Though rainfall is highly irregular and varies from year to year, the average annual precipitation tends to range between 400–600 mm on the plain, and between 800–1 200 mm in the highlands (Table 1).

The vegetation ranges from open short grassland on the plain to montane forest and heath at higher altitudes, with Acacia-Commi-

38

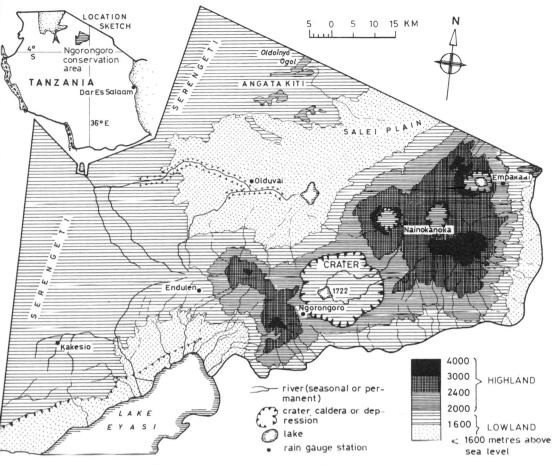

Map 4. The Ngorongoro Conservation Area.

phora woodlands on hill slopes and in the intermediary ecozones. Open and wooded grassland are the dominant vegetation types, though species composition and pasture quality vary between the plains and the highland plateaux, as well as from locality to locality within the major ecozones.

Natural water sources are unevenly distributed over the area. In general the highlands are relatively well-watered by permanent streams and springs, while the plains have few permanent water sources. In the lowlands there are no permanent streams, and during the dry season water is drawn from a few springs, pools and wells in the dry beds of seasonal rivers and from artificial water points. During the wet season surface water is plentiful all over the area. People and livestock obtain water from the many seasonal streams and rain ponds.

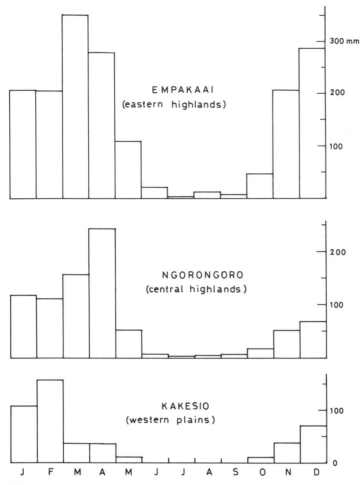

Fig. 1. Seasonal variation in rainfall in different parts of the Ngorongoro Conservation Area (monthly averages for the period 1977–79).

On the whole lowland pastures consist of short or medium-high grasses. Soils and grasses are typically rich in minerals. Grass growth is restricted to the seasonal rains, and nutritive values are highest during the wet season. Shallow soils with poor moisture reserves restrict dry season grass growth. Low standing crops mean that there is little forage available at the end of the growing season. Highland pastures, on the other hand, typically grow on deeper soils, lower in mineral content but with greater moisture reserves. A very rapid growth rate during the early rains means that nutritive values are soon diluted by less digestible cellulose. But the high standing crop of forage can support a high grazing biomass during much of the dry season.

Table 1. *Mean annual rainfall in different parts of the Ngorongoro Conservation Area*

Locality	Altitude (m)	Annual rainfall (mm)			
		Mean value 15–25 yrs[a]	Mean value 1977–79[b]	Range of variation 1973[a]	1977[a]
Nainokanoka	2 600	933	941	–	–
Ngorongoro	2 350	837	832	573	1 154
Empakaai	2 100	–	1 733	–	–
Endulen	1 830	914	1 035	663	1 131
Kakesio	1 700	–	515	–	–
Olduvai	1 500	433	443	267	642

Sources: [a] The Directorate of Meteorology, Dar es Salaam; [b] Makacha, 1980.

Apart from the distribution of water and pasture, the prevalence of livestock diseases is a major determinant of pastoral land use and settlement patterns. Livestock diseases tend to be a more serious obstacle to livestock management in the moister highlands than in the semi-arid or arid lowlands. However, none of the pastoral villages in the area is entirely free from major diseases (see Table 14, Chapter Five). East coast fever, a tick-borne disease, is reported in all villages and was said to be on the increase in 1980. Trypanosomiasis is essentially restricted to the woodland areas in the west-central, northern and extreme north-eastern parts of the area.

In sum, the natural environment of the Ngorongoro Conservation Area imposes an intricate web of constraints on land use patterns and subsistence strategies. The major resources on which the pastoralists depend for their living are unevenly distributed both in time and space. In the cool highlands, where rainfall and water sources are more reliable and the carrying capacity of the land higher than in the drier lowlands, diseases are a serious constraint in livestock management, and pastures are deficient in minerals. Conversely, on the low-lying plains, where salt and minerals are available in sufficient quantities and disease represents a minor constraint, water is scarce and unreliable, and adequate pastures are only seasonally available.

PASTORAL LAND USE AND SETTLEMENT PATTERN

The Ngorongoro Maasai seasonally utilize a wide range of habitats; plain and highland, open grassland, bushland, woodland and forest

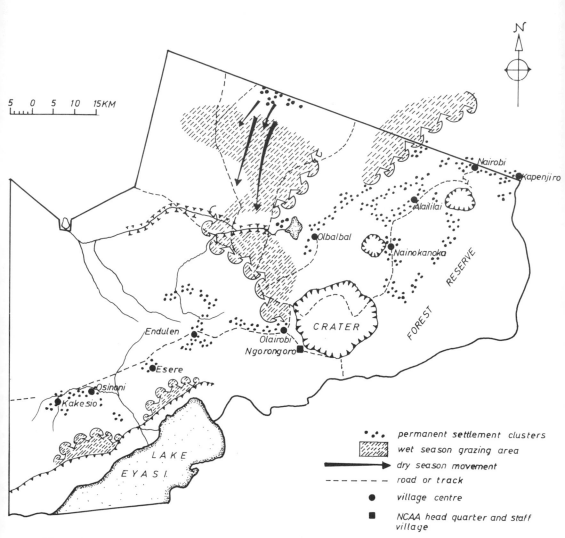

Map 5. Pastoral land use and settlement pattern in the Ngorongoro Conservation Area.

glades. Permanent, dry season settlements tend to be located near reliable water sources and adequate pastures in areas where different vegetation zones meet: at the fringe of the plains, on hill- and mountain slopes and on highland plateaux within reach of valleys and forested slopes.

The system of pastoral land use practised by the Ngorongoro Maasai can be characterized in terms of the vertical movement of livestock between highland pastures in the dry season and lowland pastures in the wet season (Map 5). The settlement pattern is mobile: people move seasonally between relatively permanent, large dry season settlements and temporary, smaller wet season camps. The movement of livestock between highland and lowland implies that pastures are seasonally allowed to recover, and that grazing pressure is distributed over a larger area and thus ideally kept at acceptable levels. For each local group of pastoralists the seasonal pastures are fairly well defined and bounded in space, so that the movement between highland and lowland pastures is a regular movement between particular areas within the locality, a movement which is practically the same from year to year.

In the dry season the population is relatively settled and concentrated to the richer grazing areas in the highlands, while it is more scattered and mobile in the wet season. Wet season camps are located near temporary water sources and flushes of green grass on the plains; the camps are shifted according to the availability of water and grass, though usually within a given area. At the onset of the rains people leave the settled area with the majority of the family herds to establish temporary camps; only a few elders and women with small children remain in the dry season settlements, with the calves and a few milking cows, throughout the year.[14]

This form of transhumant pastoralism is an efficient way of utilizing existing resources. By alternating between the highlands and lowlands, the pastoralists optimize the use of the principal resources— grass and water—at the same time as they minimize the principal constraints—the risk of disease and the scarcity of salt and minerals.

In years of average or good rains this pattern of land use enables the pastoralists to enjoy a moderate but generally adequate standard of subsistence and health, and to sell surplus stock in order to purchase the necessary minimum of consumer goods. Livestock populations tend to remain fairly stable over long periods, in balance with the local environment (cf. Jacobs, 1975). However, in periods of drought the system is upset. Pastures on the lower plains rapidly become exhausted, and people and cattle of the lowlands move up into the highlands where pastures are better preserved. Parts of the highlands tend to be set aside as refuge areas in periods of drought. People react to drought by slaughtering bulls and steers and buying agricultural foods to supplement the inadequate supplies of milk. In the worst of such years many families abandon their traditional localities and move long distances. The seasonal grazing cycle is thrown into disorder and the heavy concentration of livestock in the better highland pastures may locally cause overgrazing. The result is an accelerating loss of domestic animals which in turn means food shortage and, occasionally, famine (cf. Parkipuny, 1979).

Severe droughts recur regularly in central and northern Tanzania. Recently large parts of Tanzanian Maasailand were affected by droughts in 1960–61 and again in 1973–75. During these two drought periods, there was a marked influx of people and livestock into the Ngorongoro highlands from the surrounding lowlands with heavy pressures on the land and local disruptions of the land use patterns as a result. As will be shown below, this is reflected in the population trends in Ngorongoro over the past 20 years.

VILLAGE, WARD AND ZONE

Though traditional land use and settlement patterns prevail in the Ngorongoro Conservation Area, they are subject to administrative and political controls exercised by the state through the Conservation Authority and the local political party (CCM) branches. The Ngorongoro Conservation Area is divided into three administrative zones, four wards and nine registered villages. The villages of Kakesio, Osinoni, Endulen and Esere form the Western Zone; the villages of Olairobi and Olbalbal-Meshili form the Central Zone, which also includes the scattered pastoral settlements of the Oldoinyo Oogol mountains in the north; and the villages of Nainokanoka, Alaililai and Nairobi (Nayobi) form the Eastern Zone. At the extreme north-eastern corner of the Conservation Area is the village of Kapenjiro, which is not yet registered as a pastoral village in the Conservation Area. The villages in the Central Zone constitute one ward, the villages in the Eastern Zone another. The Western Zone is divided into two wards, one formed by the Kakesio and Osinoni villages, the other by the villages of Endulen and Esere (see Map 5).

The Western Zone stretches from the Serengeti plain and the woodlands of the Eyasi Escarpment to the western foothills of the Ngorongoro highlands. The Central Zone includes the Ngorongoro highlands, the Olbalbal depression and the dry plains and hills of the northern part of the Conservation Area, while the Eastern Zone comprises the Melenda high plateau and the Empakaai highlands.

The formation of villages and wards as administrative units was the result of the villagization programme of the mid 1970s. The village centres were located in or near previously existing trading centres, such as Kakesio, Endulen, Olairobi, Olbalbal and Nainokanoka. Dispensaries, primary schools and village shops were established where there were none before. But in terms of the actual concentration of settlements, the villagization programme in Ngorongoro was a failure. It did not significantly alter the established patterns of settlement and land use. Minor adjustments and movements took place. Some settlements were shifted short distances to conform to prescribed village layouts—lines of settlements along the roads or circular concentrations around trading centres. The most drastic interventions were the expulsion of the pastoral settlements from the Ngorongoro Crater (see Chapter Three above) and the concentration of the scattered pastoral population in the hilly drylands of Oldoinyo Oogol. The Oldoinyo Oogol Maasai resisted villagization because they felt that the land could not carry the concentration of people and herds. The authorities reacted by burning their houses and kraal camps and driving away the people from their homes. Today, however, many of the people moved by force have returned to their old settlement sites and grazing grounds.

The concept of village stands in this context for a political and administrative unit imposed upon the pastoralists by the state. As a social and economic unit it means little or nothing to the people inhabiting it. The physical and legal boundaries of the village usually do not coincide with the boundaries of the traditional political and social units (inkutot) which are still meaningful and operative among the Ngorongoro Maasai. And in terms of the system of resource utilization the village tends to be a non-viable unit. Physically the village simply consists of a trading centre with shops, a school, perhaps a dispensary and a nucleus of mud or brick houses mainly inhabited by non-Maasai shopkeepers, school teachers and administrative officials. The pastoral settlements tend to be widely scattered throughout the village land, many settlements being located 10 km or more away from the centre.

If villagization thus did not bring about significant changes in the settlement and land use patterns in Ngorongoro, it did, however, bring a new political structure to the pastoral community. But the new leadership structure, the village government, was added to the traditional authority structure rather than replacing it. Both structures came to operate side by side in different political spheres, in many respects complementing rather than contradicting each other. The village government thus deals with the relations between villagers and the external authorities—the district authority and the Conservation Authority—while internal conflicts between families in the village —disputes over livestock transactions and marriage—are still dealt with through the traditional political channels. In most villages the traditional leaders have in fact assumed the functions of the new village government; an influential age-set leader is also the village chairman or secretary, and the "ten-cell" leaders are invariably the settlement heads, the members of the traditional council of elders.

PEOPLE AND LIVESTOCK:
RECENT POPULATION TRENDS

The 1978 national census gives a figure of 17982 pastoral inhabitants in the Ngorongoro Conservation Area. A review of earlier census material reveals a pattern of significant fluctuations. A population of 10633 in 1957 dropped to 5435 in 1970 and then steadily increased until 1978. There are no official census figures available thereafter, but the settlement count in the late dry season of 1980 indicates a trend of moderate population decrease since 1978. Thus the number of pastoral settlements dropped fron 791 in 1978 to 691 in 1980. This would suggest a pastoral population of some 14600 individuals in 1980 (cf. Århem, 1981 a).

The apparent population decrease between 1978–80 is in line with the information on population movements in the Conservation Area: a survey in 1980 revealed that far more people had left the Conservation Area than entered it during the last two years of the decade (Århem, 1981 a: 35). The major reason for this emigration was, according to the pastoralists themselves, a growing food shortage due to decreasing family herds, the prohibition on agriculture and the poor distribution of grain in the area (ibid; see also Chapter Five below). It is also likely that many of the pastoralists who left Ngorongoro in the late 1970s were people who had moved into the Ngorongoro highlands from the surrounding lowlands during the severe drought in the mid 1970s. They were, in other words, returning home.

The population trends for domestic livestock in the Conservation Area closely parallel those of the human population. With minor oscillations from year to year, the cattle population showed a steady decrease from 161034 animals in 1960 to 64766 in 1970. Then the population increased to 123609 in 1974. Between 1974 and 1980 the population level was relatively stable. The 1980 livestock census gives a cattle population of 118358 in the Ngorongoro Conservation Area.

The picture is similar for small stock, except for a steady decline in numbers from 1977. From a figure of 100689 in 1960, the small stock population dropped, with minor oscillations, to 41866 in 1970. It then drastically increased to 157568 in 1974—a threefold increase in three years—and reached a highest point of 244831 in 1977. The population then dropped to an estimated 144675 in the 1980 livestock census (Fig 2; Table 2).

These figures should, however, be regarded with some caution in light of the fact that the pastoral population—and particularly the herds of domestic stock—are mobile; settlements change location seasonally and in accordance with major climatic fluctuations. It may

Table 2. *Human and livestock population trends in the Ngorongoro Conservation Area 1957–80*

| Year | People[a] | Cattle | Small stock | |
			Goats	Sheep
1957	10 633[b]			
1960		161 034	100 689	
1962		142 230	83 120	
1964		132 490	82 980	
1966	8 728	94 580	68 590	
1968		103 568	71 196	
1970[c]	5 435	64 766	17 621	24 245
1974	12 645	123 609	56 225	101 343
1978	17 982	107 838	91 628	95 357
1980	14 645[d]	118 358	144 675	

[a] Refers to the pastoral population.
[b] Refers to the pastoral population in the Serengeti-Ngorongoro area before the creation of the Serengeti National Park and the Ngorongoro Conservation Area.
[c] All census figures from 1970 are extremely low and should be treated with caution.
[d] Estimation based on the 1980 settlement count (see Århem 1981 a).
Source: Official statistics from the NCAA.

thus be the case that settlements temporarily have moved into or out of the Conservation Area at the time of the census. The censuses are therefore not always strictly comparable from year to year, particularly as not all censuses were taken during the same season. Especially the small stock figures must be considered very approximate as small stock are extremely mobile, and seasonally tend to be divided up and scattered for management purposes between different settlements or kraal camps, some of which may be located inside the boundaries of the Conservation Area while others may be situated outside it. These circumstances introduce a measure of uncertainty and a considerable margin of error in the population statistics (cf. Århem, 1981 a).[15]

Yet, certain general and significant trends and patterns emerge in the statistical material, which are summarized in the following:

1. Both human and livestock populations have fluctuated according to a regular pattern. The available information on rainfall and pasture conditions in the Conservation Area between 1960 and 1980 suggest that the fluctuations are due to large scale population movements in and out of the Conservation Area in response to alternations between periods of drought and abundant or adequate rainfall (Århem, 1981 a; Dirschl, 1966). In the very dry years of 1960–61 and

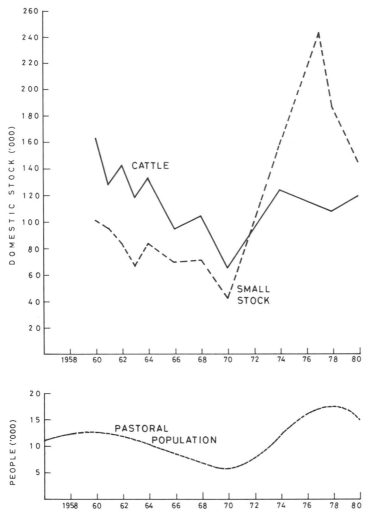

Fig. 2. Human and livestock population trends in the Ngorongoro Conservation Area 1957–80.

1974–75, people and livestock from the lowlands surrounding Ngorongoro moved into the Ngorongoro highlands. In the years of relatively abundant rainfall following upon the two drought periods, the majority of the immigrants returned with their stock to the areas from which they came. The pastoralists generally respond to periods of high rainfall by moving away from the highland pastures and out onto the plains where pastures are richer and the disease risk smaller. It should perhaps be added that the pastoralists themselves attributed the low population levels in the late 1960s to the 1967 eruption of the active volcano Oldoinyo Lengai in the north-eastern corner of the

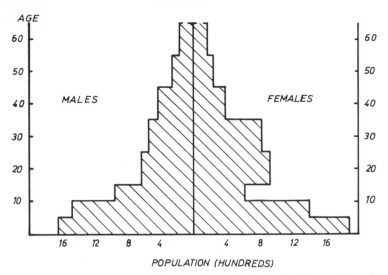

Fig. 3. The structure of the pastoral population in the Ngorongoro Conservation Area, 1978.

Conservation Area: as the ash from the eruption was brought westward by the prevailing winds, covering large areas of grazingland, the people and their herds migrated outside the Conservation Area in search of better pastures (cf. Fosbrooke, 1972: 39).

2. Though human and livestock populations have fluctuated over the past 20 years, the level of the human population was higher in 1980 than in 1960. This suggests a moderate natural increase—independent of the drought-induced population movements—near the regional average (around 2–2.5%; cf. Kurji, 1981 *a* and Århem, 1981 *a*). The age-sex structure of the pastoral population in the Conservation Area (1978) is shown in Fig. 3. Children under 15 constitute some 45% of the total population, and the proportion of women between 15–44 is about 24%. The crude birth rate among the Ngorongoro Maasai has been estimated to 3.0% per year (Kurji, 1981 *a*: 19).[16] This picture agrees well with that of other pastoral populations in East Africa: pastoralists tend to have a relatively low fertility rate—comparatively lower than agricultural populations—and a slow to moderate natural increase rate (Little, 1980). The relative stability or moderate growth rate of pastoral populations is related to institutionalized mechanisms of population control built into the social system as well as natural checks and balances. The age discrepancy between males and females at marriage and the high marriage age of males resulting from the Maasai age-set system, and the sexual restraint prescribed for women during the long period of breast feeding are such cultural mechanisms of population control among East

Table 3. *Changes in herd composition and livestock per capita ratios in Ngorongoro, 1960–80*

	1960	1963	1966	1970	1974	1978	1980
Cattle per capita	12.6		10.8	11.9	9.7	6.0	
Small stock per capita	7.9		7.9	7.7	12.5	10.4	
Percentage small stock of total herd	38	36	42	39	56	63	55

Source: Statistics from the NCAA (see also Århem, 1981 a).

African pastoralists, still very much in operation among the Ngorongoro Maasai.

3. The growth of the human population in Ngorongoro is not accompanied by a corresponding growth in the cattle herd. The total cattle herd was substantially larger in the early 1960s than in the mid and late 1970s. The implication is that the ratio of cattle per capita in Ngorongoro has fallen drastically—from approximately 13 head of cattle in 1960 to six in 1978 (Table 3). This, in turn, implies a radical change in the pastoral economy during the period (dealt with in Chapter Five below).

4. The decline in size of the total cattle herd is functionally related to the substantial growth of the small stock herd since 1970. The small stock herd was considerably larger in the mid and late 1970s than in the early 1960s. There has, in other words, been a radical change in the composition of the total livestock herd in Ngorongoro during the past 20 years (see Table 3). The proportion of small stock has increased from 38% of the total livestock herd in 1960, to 55% in 1980, with a peak of 69% in 1977. The increase in size of the small stock herd must be seen as a strategy of the pastoral household to make up for the decline in the cattle herd, and the falling ratio of cattle per capita. Small stock have increasingly become a substitute for cattle in the pastoral economy of the Ngorongoro Maasai. The pastoral econo-

Table 4. *Human and livestock population densities in the Ngorongoro Conservation Area 1960–1980*

	1960	1966	1970	1974	1978	1980
Pastoral Population		1.2	0.8	1.8	2.6	2.1
Cattle	23.1	13.5	9.3	17.7	15.4	16.9
Small stock	14.4	9.8	6.0	22.5	26.7	20.7

Source: Statistics from the NCAA (cf. Århem 1981 a).

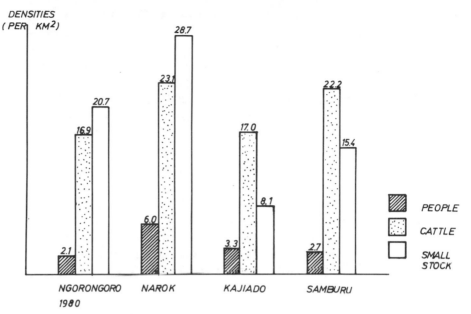

Fig. 4. Variations in human and livestock population densities in different pastoral areas of East Africa.

my has changed from a cattle-based to a small stock-dependent livestock economy. This implies a process of impoverishment, and it is experienced as such by the Ngorongoro Maasai themselves. Yet, it should be pointed out that the trend appears to be reverting after 1977. The pastoral population is levelling off, while the number of cattle is increasing and the number of small stock again falling. In other words, the pastoral economy seems to be on its way to recovery after a crisis in the mid 1970s; a crisis which was triggered by the severe drought at the time.

POPULATION DENSITY, STOCKING RATE AND THE CARRYING CAPACITY OF THE LAND

The density of the pastoral population and the stocking rates of the domestic livestock in the Ngorongoro Conservation Area fall well within the range of average values for other pastoral areas in East Africa (Table 4 and Fig. 4). Over the past 20 years the pastoral population density in Ngorongoro has varied between approximately one and three persons per square km. The stocking rate for cattle varied over the same period between nine and 23 head of cattle per square km, while the small stock density varied between six and 27 (Table 4). The pastoral population density in Ngorongoro in 1980 was

51

2.1 as compared with a density ranging between 2.7–6.0 in a sample of pastoral populations in Kenya (Fig. 4, based on data in Dyson-Hudson, 1980: 180). The stocking rate for cattle in Ngorongoro in 1980 was 16.9, which comes close to the corresponding values from the Kenyan sample: stocking rates for cattle here varied between 17–23 with the highest rate in Narok district (ibid). The highest cattle densities in Ngorongoro obtained during the drought periods 1960–61 and 1974–75 when pastoralists from the more severely affected lowlands moved into the drought refuges in the Ngorongoro highlands, with a high livestock concentration in Ngorongoro as a result.

The optimal stocking rate for domestic livestock—a crude but useful measure of pastoral carrying capacity—in the entire Ngorongoro Conservation Area has been estimated to 102 000 standard livestock units (Fosbrooke, 1972: 192). This figure is calculated on 1 000 pound animal units and an area of 7 000 square km available for grazing (allowing for variations in carrying capacity according to different habitat types).

The total domestic stocking rate (including both cattle and small stock, converted into standard livestock units) is slightly lower in 1980 than in 1961: approximately 84 000 units as compared with 87 000 units in 1961. The present domestic stocking rate thus falls well below the estimated optimal carrying capacity of the area. In this perspective the fluctuations in the livestock populations over the past two decades appear as oscillations around the optimal stocking rate for the area. In periods of drought, when the carrying capacity is reduced and large populations concentrate in the highlands, the stocking rate approaches or locally exceeds the carrying capacity of the land. Starvation and disease follow, with a decrease in livestock numbers and a reduction of grazing pressure as a result. In better years people and livestock disperse and the land is allowed to recover. This pattern characterized the periods during and after the two major droughts in 1960–61 and 1974–75.

It is possible to specify the relationship between the actual stocking rate and the pastoral carrying capacity of the Conservation Area further. By breaking down the Conservation Area into distinct dry season ranges, and using an alternative method of estimating the carrying capacity of natural pastures developed by Coe et al. (1976), a more differentiated picture emerges which reinforces the overall picture of the pastoral ecosystem in Ngorongoro presented above. The formulas developed by Coe and his collaborators assume a predictive relationship between mean annual precipitation and large herbivore biomass. Applied to the data from Ngorongoro they yield Table 5. It should be stressed that all values in the table are approximate. The predictive relationship between large herbivore biomass and rainfall

Table 5. *Actual stocking rate in relation to estimated carrying capacity in different parts of the Ngorongoro Conservation Area 1980*

	Estimated rainfall (mm/year)	Actual biomass of domestic stock (kg/km^2)	Estimated total carrying capacity (kg/km^2)
Oldonyo Oogol	435	2 019	2 400
Kakesio	500	2 486	2 970
Olbalbal	650	3 471	4 790
Endulen	900	3 898	8 220
Olairobi (Central Highlands)	900	10 073	8 220
Melenda (Eastern Highlands)	1 100	10 532	11 800

Note: The calculation of actual biomass is based or Århem (1981 a: 33). The estimates of carrying capacity are based on Coe et al. (1976).

principally refers to wildlife ecosystems, and particularly to areas which receive less than 700 mm rainfall per year. Furthermore, it refers to total (dry and wet season) ranges utilized by grazing herbivores. The estimates of actual biomass in different parts of the Conservation Area in the table refer, however, only to domestic stock and dry season ranges. Nevertheless, the information in Table 5 agrees well with the other evidence presented in this report: actual stocking rates vary in proportion to annual precipitation and are generally lower than the estimated carrying capacity. Only in Olairobi (central highlands) does the stocking rate exceed the estimated capacity, while it falls well below it in Endulen—one of the principal emigration zones in the Conservation Area.

THE ENVIRONMENTAL IMPACT

These tentative conclusions are supported by independent evidence on recent vegetation changes in the area. A study by King (1983) shows that erosion and grassland deterioration are very localized. Since 1970, the destruction of vegetation has been most intensive during the drought in the mid 1970s, and it was particularly marked in areas of great stock concentrations—in Olduvai where water was available throughout the drought period and in parts of the Melenda plateau. Normal geological erosion occurs on the sandy and unstable soils of the Kakesio plain, and a belt of sand dunes is steadily spreading southwestward from the northern part of the Sale plain outside the boundaries of the Conservation Area. The cause of the spreading sand dunes is not known but may be related to the combination of dry season grazing by domestic stock and the heavy utilization of the Sale plain in the wet season by increasing numbers of wildebeest (ibid; see also below).

The unpalatable and coarse buffalo grass (*Eleusine jaegeri*) is spreading in the highland areas of Ngorongoro and Melenda. The cause of this expansion is again not clear, though range management officers at the Conservation Authority relate it to overgrazing by domestic stock. That this cannot be the sole cause is, however, clear from the fact that the grass is spreading also in areas which are not, or only little, grazed by domestic stock—for example, in the Olmoti Crater and in the Forest Reserve (cf. Fosbrooke, 1972: 61). A more plausible explanation has been proposed by Branagan (1974). According to him, the expansion of unpalatable grasses in the highlands is, in part, a consequence of the ban on grass burning in the Conservation Area since the early 1960s. Where previously unpalatable grasses were kept at bay by burning, they now expand over the entire highland plateau, suppressing the palatable grasses, and thus radically reducing the dry season pastures. The spread of the tall and coarse grasses in the highlands also led to an increase in the incidence of tick-borne diseases, as ticks thrive in the tall, moist highland grasses (ibid). Whatever the causes, the spread of the buffalo grass does not, however, in any way imply a degradation of the soil in a strictly biological perspective. On the contrary, it enhances the water-holding capacity of the soil and reduces the risk of erosion by preventing trampling and removal of the grass cover.

Destruction of forest vegetation is at present negligible and has decreased notably since 1975, when agriculture was prohibited in Ngorongoro. The forest destruction which occurred before 1975 was restricted to areas of cultivated land—particularly around Endulen and in the Empakaai highlands (Kikula, 1983). It should be noted here that these were the areas inhabited by relatively large groups of non-Maasai cultivators, many of whom left the Conservation Area after the prohibition of agriculture (cf. Chapter Three above, and Chapter Five below). The overall conclusion is that pastoral land use in Ngorongoro has had little destructive impact on vegetation over the past 20 years. The impact has been localized and periodic: periods of relatively significant impact, in the form of overgrazing and trampling in areas of high stock concentration during very dry years, are followed by periods of insignificant impact during years of abundant or average rainfall, when livestock are dispersed and pastures are allowed to recover.

Shifting the focus from an examination of the impact of pastoralism

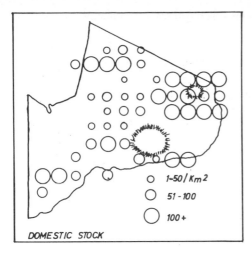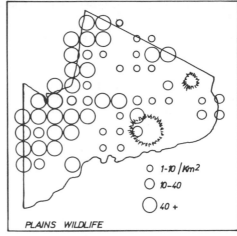

Based on Ecosystems Report, 1980

Map 6. Distribution and density of domestic stock and plains wildlife in the Ngorongoro Conservation Area, February 1980.

on vegetation to the interaction between wildlife and domestic stock, a more disconcerting picture emerges. However, the picture is disconcerting from the point of view not of wildlife conservation, but of the pastoralists. Thus, while the total herd of domestic stock in Ngorongoro has decreased over the past 20 years, the total population of wild ungulates—particularly wildebeest—has drastically increased in numbers during the same period. Between 1970 and 1980 the total Serengeti wildebeest population more than doubled. It increased from an estimated 650 000 to 1.8 million in 1980, implying an annual growth rate of about 11% (Ecosystems Report, 1980; Sinclair, 1979; Babu, 1981). Accompanying this population explosion was a change in its migratory behaviour. Millions of wildebeest now penetrate deep into the Ngorongoro Conservation Area during the wet season each year.

The distribution of plains wildlife and domestic stock in the Conservation Area during the wet season 1980 is shown in Map 6. It shows that there was relatively little overlap in the distribution of plains wildlife, particularly wildebeest, and domestic stock: the pastoralists avoid mingling their herds with the migrating wildebeest during this time of the year—the calving period of the wildebeest—because the wildebeest calves transmit malignant catarrhal fever to the cattle. The pastoralists exposed to the wildebeest migration are thus forced to retreat up into the hills and highlands, traditionally reserved only for dry season use, in order to evade the disease risk. In this way the eruption of the wildebeest population has disrupted the pastoral land use pattern in parts of the Conservation Area (Parkipuny, 1983). In

55

Table 6. *Plains ungulates in the Serengeti ecosystem: Population trends 1961–78*

Species	1961[a]	1965	1970[a]	1975[a]	1978[b]
Wildebeest	260 000	439 000[a]	640 000	1 100 000	1 500 000
Zebra	165 000	200 000[a]	150 000		200 000
Thomsons gazelle		600 000[c]			700 000
Grants gazelle		40 000[c]	30 000		50 000
Buffalo	23 000	41 000[c]	60 000	73 000	74 000
Impala		10 000[c]			75 000
Eland		5 000[c]			18 000

Sources: [a] Sinclair, 1979; [b] Babu, 1981; [c] Fosbrooke, 1972.

other parts and at other times of the year, however, domestic stock and plains wildlife intermingle relatively freely, and their utilization of range resources is complementary rather than competitive. In fact, domsetic stock and wild grazing ungulates tend—under traditional forms of extensive grazing on natural pastures—to utilize different food resources and occupy different positions in the grazing chain, thus facilitating energy flow from one species to another (Jewell, 1980; Bell, 1971).

The eruption of the wildebeest population is believed to be a consequence of the extermination of rinderpest in domestic stock in the 1940s, and a series of good rains in the northern part of Serengeti—the dry season ground for wildebeest—in the 1960s and early 1970s (Sinclair, 1979). It may also be related to the expulsion of the pastoralists and their herds of domestic stock in Serengeti, and the consequent elimination of the competition over pastures and water previously checking both the wild and domestic livestock populations (Table 6).

SUMMARY

When the study, on which this Chapter is based, was anticipated and carried out in 1980–81, it was widely believed within the Ngorongoro Conservation Area Authority that the human and domestic livestock populations in the area were steadily increasing, and surpassing the carrying capacity of the land. The material presented in the Chapter has shown that this is not the case. Livestock population levels tend to fluctuate around an optimal level in terms of the estimated carrying capacity of the land. There is no reason for immediate concern about environmental degradation in the Ngorongoro Conservation Area, nor does it seem likely that the present system of pastoral land use will have a negative effect on wildlife and vegetation in the foreseeable future. Indeed, the Ngorongoro Conservation Area seems to be one of the very few areas in Tanzania in which the pastoral ecosystem has been able to maintain until the present a dynamic equilibrium, and in which the transhumant pattern of land use is still operative on a traditional basis. To a great extent this is due to the fact that the Ngorongoro Maasai have been spared large scale agricultural encroachment and massive land alienation. Though the conservation regime in Ngorongoro has imposed restrictions on the pastoralists, it has also protected them from the worst effects of the pressure for land by the agricultural peoples outside the Conservation Area.

However, the area is not without its problems. But these problems are of an economic rather than an environmental nature, and of immediate concern to the pastoralists rather than to the Conservation Authority. Over the past two decades there has been a considerable decline in the cattle per capita ratio in the area. This trend becomes even clearer when the census figures available from 1929 and 1954 are taken into account (see Chapter Three above). In a fifty-year perspective, the human population of the Conservation Area has grown in absolute terms, while the cattle (and small stock) population has decreased. In an ecological perspective the cattle population appears remarkably stable over time, but the economic implications of the falling per capita ratio of cattle are significant: the Ngorongoro Maasai have become poorer, their subsistence standard has declined.

Plate 1. Boy (*olayoni*) with herd.

Plate 2. Young man (*olmorani*) with herd.

Plate 3. Permanent settlement (*enkang*).

Plate 4. Outside the house.

Plate 5. Milking in the morning.

Plate 6. Watering cattle at the hot spring in Esere.

Plate 7. Family on the move along the Oldogom River (dry season, 1984).

Plate 8. Lion feeding on his kill—a zebra.

Plate 9. Wildebeest in the Ngorongoro Crater.

Plate 10. Kakesio village.

Plate 11. Women fetching water from the communal tap in Olbalbal village.

5. Living Conditions Among the Ngorongoro Maasai

This Chapter provides an outline of the overall socioeconomic situation of the Ngorongoro Maasai. It aims to assess the development needs and priorities of the pastoral community in Ngorongoro. To this end it describes the material conditions of life in Ngorongoro in terms of a series of concrete variables including housing, property, food, health and income. Community services such as schools, dispensaries, water supplies, veterinary services, shops and markets are mapped and discussed in relation to these variables. Particular attention is paid to major changes in living conditions over the past two decades.

HOUSING AND MATERIAL POSSESSIONS

The Ngorongoro Maasai seasonally occupy two types of settlements: the relatively permanent dry season settlement and the temporary and smaller wet season camp. In Ngorongoro the large majority of pastoral settlements, both permanent and temporary, are of the traditional Maasai type. The permanent settlement (*enkang* or *enkang emparnat*) is seasonally inhabited from year to year. It is built for permanent use, with a high kraal fence and solid houses made of poles and slats tied together by bark strips and covered with a plaster of cowdung which is regularly renewed. In contrast, the temporary camp (*ronjo* or *parrimangat*) usually consists of a hastily built thorn fence around a few small and simple huts made of poles and sticks, covered with grass and hides rather than cowdung. The temporary camp is rebuilt every year and usually shifts location from year to year. It is not uncommon to find a camp shifting place several times during a single season according to the availability of water and pasture.

The permanent settlement consists of a circle of houses surrounded by a thornbush fence for the protection of the livestock. The livestock are kept in the open space at the centre of the settlement during the night. The house (*enkaji*), entirely built by women, is oval or oblong in shape, with a relatively flat roof. It has one low entrance leading into a large room. A fireplace in the centre provides light in the otherwise dark and smoky room. At one side is a screened-off compartment reserved for the housewife and her small children. At the opposite side is another compartment, or simply a broad bed-shelf, for other house members and guests. The beds, covered with layers of hides, are built on wooden frames above the hard stamped mud floor. Often there is a third compartment near the entrance, divided off from the main room by a screen or wall, in which newborn calves and lambs are kept at night.

Permanent settlements change site and new houses are built every three to five years. Some settlements may be continuously occupied much longer, up to 10 years. Shifts tend to be local: a new settlement is usually built adjacent to an old one. The accumulation of dung in the kraal is one reason for the frequent shift of settlements. The mobile (transhumant) pattern of settlement puts certain restrictions on the form, size and construction of the house: construction material must be easily and locally available, and the house must be relatively rapidly completed. Sanitary practices are simple but functional in the semi-arid environment. People urinate at the back of the houses and go to specific places in the bush, away from the settlements, for defecation. Household wastes, mainly consisting of bones and other organic material, are disposed of at the back of the houses or, again, outside the settlement.

The modest appearance of the houses, the elementary sanitary practices and the fact that people and livestock virtually share living space are usually seen by administrators and planners as an indication of extreme poverty. However, this entirely negative view of the traditional Maasai settlement overlooks a number of its adaptive advantages. On the whole, the Maasai settlement is carefully and solidly built. Houses are constructed in accordance with well-defined indigenous standards of design, developed in response to the exigencies of the savanna environment and the pastoral mode of life. They are endowed with a profound affective value and cultural significance. The design of the house—the small, s-shaped entrance corridor, the darkness and smoke inside—keeps it entirely free from flies which abound outside. The smoke from the fireplace and the insulated walls of slats, grass and cowdung, keep the house dry and provide a relatively constant temperature inside—cool during the hot days and warm during the chilly nights.

At the present low population density, the lack of latrines hardly constitutes a health problem. People attend to their needs away from the living space of the settlement and away from its water sources. The semi-arid climate quickly dries out feces and other organic wastes. The ever-present flies and the cowdung cover in the kraal pose more of a sanitary problem, particularly during the rains. Flies transmit eye diseases which are prevalent among the pastoralists—a problem made more serious by the scarcity of surface water which puts restrictions on cleanliness. During the rains the cowdung layer turns into a thick, smelly mud, which increases the disease risk among livestock as well as people. The Ngorongoro Maasai respond to this situation by either moving to a new settlement site, or by removing and burning the cowdung every dry season.

Material possessions are scarce in the pastoral household. This is obviously a function of the transhumant pattern of settlement and land use. Seasonal migrations do not allow for the accumulation of material possessions. Nor are they necessary. Food, and raw materials for most household goods and clothing are provided by the livestock. Nature provides for other necessities, including firewood and wood for house construction. Each household possesses a minimum inventory of household goods which varies little from household to household. Economic differentiation is rather reflected in the size of the polygynous family and the family herd. The basic inventory of goods encountered in most pastoral households consists of the traditional milk gourds and calebass containers, leather bags for carrying grain, leather skirts and belts, knives and spears forged by Maasai smiths, tin containers for water, cooking pots, cups and spoons and usually some blankets and pieces of cloth (shuka). A great variety of bead work is used as adornment. Beads are bought in market places and made into collars, armlets and ankle rings by women, or they are obtained ready-made at the market.

Household goods and cloth are used for long periods and only replaced when utterly worn out or unusable. Cash returns from livestock sales are not converted into a broader range of possessions, improved housing or the like, but are spent on the purchase of grain, livestock or the basic household goods mentioned above. This pattern of consumption among the Ngorongoro Maasai reflects their subsistence-oriented pastoral economy, but also the limited supply of commodities in the villages.

LIVESTOCK HOLDINGS

The most fundamental and valued property of the pastoral Maasai is their livestock. Cattle are considered the supreme value, and small stock are largely seen as a substitute for cattle. As was shown in Chapter Four above, livestock herds in Ngorongoro have declined in size over the past 50 years, and the composition of the herds changed considerably between 1960 and 1980. The cattle per capita ratio has fallen while the proportion of small stock in the total herd has risen. Forsbrooke (1972: 193) has stated that the Maasai traditionally strove to maintain a proportion of small stock of about 35% of the total herd. The data presented in Chapter Four (Table 3) reveal that the Ngorongoro Maasai roughly managed to maintain this ratio throughout the 1960s, but that the proportion of small stock thereafter rose to 55–65% in the 1970s. Small stock have become increasingly important in the pastoral economy, in this case indicating a process of impoverishment. The cattle-based pastoral economy of the Ngorongoro Maasai has changed into a small-stock dependent economy.

Several authors have attempted to estimate the minimum herd necessary to sustain a family in a subsistence-oriented pastoral economy. Jewell (1980:372) estimates that an average pastoral family of eight persons (on a diet based 75% on milk) needs a minimum herd of 44 head of cattle and some 100 small stock, which means between five and six head of cattle and 12–13 small stock per capita. This is a low estimate. Other estimates are considerably higher. Dahl and Hjort (1976) estimate that a minimum herd of 67 head of cattle provides the necessary energy and protein for a family of five adult equivalents, which gives a ratio of almost 13 head of cattle per adult equivalent or about 10 head of cattle per capita. This value is comparable with Jewell's values for cattle and small stock taken together.

On the basis of Dahl and Hjort's figures, Kjaerby (1979) has attempted to calculate the minimum herd in an exchange-oriented, partly commercialized, pastoral economy. By exchange-oriented pastoralism he means a pastoral economy in which livestock is exchanged for grain in order to supplement the purely pastoral diet with agricultural foods. Kjaerby assumes a situation where the calorie requirements are met by the purchase of grain while the protein requirements are met solely by the consumption of milk and meat from the family herds, and in which the barter terms of trade are set at 450 kg maize flour per head of cattle. This is a hypothetical situation which, in fact, comes very close to the current (1980) economic reality in the Ngorongoro Conservation Area (cf. Table 11 below). Kjaerby estimates that a family of 7.1 adult equivalents needs a herd of 46 head of cattle to meet its subsistence requirements, which translates into approximately five head of cattle per capita.

Jacobs (1975) gives a figure of 14 head of cattle as the average livestock holding for the pastoral Maasai in the 1960s. This average, which refers to subsistence-oriented, pure pastoralism, is considerably higher than the minimum values for the subsistence herd given above, and substantiates Jacobs' contention that the pastoral Maasai traditionally were one of the richest cattle owning peoples in Africa. The data from Ngorongoro showed that the cattle per capita ratio among the Ngorongoro Maasai has fallen from about 13 in 1960 to six in 1978. In light of the discussion of the pastoral minimum herd above, this means that the level of subsistence among the Ngorongoro Maasai has fallen from a level of relative prosperity by any pastoral standards to one of bare subsistence.

The changes in herd composition and cattle per capita in Ngorongoro over the past 20 years have been accompanied by another process of change with profound social and economic implications: a tendency towards increasing economic differentiation among the pastoralists. The gap between rich and poor livestock owners has widened, and the number of very poor households has grown. Surveys in 1980–81 revealed that some 15% of the pastoral households have less than 10 head of cattle, which is far below the subsistence minimum, while less than 5% have more than 300 head of cattle, which is well above it. The large majority of pastoralists own a herd of some 30–50 animals, which implies that they barely manage to subsist on the offtake from their herds and the exchange of livestock for grain (Århem, 1981 b). While the richer herd owners are capable of maintaining or increasing their herds and hence are less dependent on livestock sales for the purchase of grain, the poorer herd owners are forced to sell their livestock at a rate detrimental to herd reproduction in order to obtain grain.

THE PROBLEM OF AGRICULTURE

The current living conditions of the Ngorongoro Maasai, particularly their food situation, are intimately connected with the question of agriculture in Ngorongoro. Due to the weakening of the pastoral economy over the past 20 years, the prohibition on agriculture has become a critical, indeed the major, problem to the Ngorongoro Maasai. Until 1975 agriculture was permitted in parts of the Ngorongoro Conservation Area. When the Conservation Area was created in 1959 there were already many cultivators established in Endulen, Kakesio and the Empakaai area. Most cultivators were not Maasai; they were Arusha, Iraqw and Sukuma. The shopkeepers and traders of Asian and Somali origin in the trading centres had substantial areas under cultivation, particularly in Endulen and Kakesio. But, there was also a considerable number of pastoral Maasai who took up cultivation as a supplementary line of subsistence production in the 1960s and early 1970s. It is difficult to assess the actual number of Maasai households which were engaged in subsistence cultivation, since no survey of the extent and impact of agriculture in Ngorongoro has ever been carried out. Moreover, it is clear that many Maasai pastoralists had small gardens in the vicinity of their pastoral settlements which were cultivated by non-Maasai agriculturalists—usually

Table 7. *The importance of agriculture in the Ngorongoro Conservation Area before its prohibition in 1975*

	Estimated percentage of total number of settlements in different villages engaged in small-scale cultivation		
	−25 %	25–75 %	75 %–
Kakesio			×
Esere		×	
Endulen			×
Olairobi	×		
Olbalbal			×
Nainokanoka			×
Alaililai			×
Nairobi			×

Source: Own survey 1980.

Iraqw—working on a sort of share cropping basis. Table 7 gives a very approximate picture of the importance of agriculture in the Conservation Area in the years before 1975. Note that no distinction is made between pastoral households working their own plots and households involved in a share cropping arrangement with non-Maasai cultivators. It can, however, be concluded that in the mid 1970s agriculture was an important subsistence activity among the Ngorongoro Maasai, and that agriculture provided an important source of supplementary foods for the pastoralists (Århem, 1981 c).

The crops cultivated varied between highland and lowland. In the lowlands, it was essentially maize, supplemented by various types of vegetables. In the highlands, maize was combined with beans, potatoes and cabbage. The gardens were small, most of them less than an acre and only a few were as large as five acres. In fact, most gardens seem to have been confined to old or abandoned settlement sites. The larger farms were owned and managed by non-Maasai people, who subsisted on agriculture rather than pastoralism.

Agriculture was prohibited in 1975 because the Ngorongoro Conservation Area Authority felt that cultivation was getting out of control. Cultivation had spread up to the eastern rim of the Ngorongoro Crater, there were cultivated plots in the Empakaai Crater, and cultivation extended over an ever widening area in the Endulen ward. The Conservation Authority feared that the Ngorongoro environment was threatened. This fear was articulated during the "conservation controversy" in the late 1960s, but the definite legal decision to

69

prohibit agriculture was delayed by persistent opposition from local pastoralists and cultivators, backed by local as well as national politicians (see Chapter Three above).

Two points are worth noting about the 1975 decision. The first is that few effective administrative actions were taken to control and restrict agriculture prior to the complete prohibition. Secondly, the most immediate environmental threat was posed by the non-Maasai farmers residing in the Conservation Area. As a result of the prohibition most of these farmers left the area. Today the only substantial non-Maasai population in Ngorongoro is to be found in the villages of Nairobi and Kapenjiro in the Empakaai highlands, where approximately 60% of the population are WaArusha (Århem, 1981 a).

Another, and perhaps more serious effect of the ban on agriculture in Ngorongoro was an acutely felt shortage of agricultural foods in the area. The prohibition deepened and accentuated the ill feeling existing among the pastoralists towards the Conservation Authority. This reaction can only be understood against the background of the pastoralists' longstanding and consistent dependence upon agricultural foods as a supplement to their pastoral foods. Throughout the history of the Serengeti-Ngorongoro area the Maasai pastoralists have depended, to a greater or lesser exent, on access to agricultural foods, and on the exchange of livestock and pastoral products for grain. It was this dependence, expressed in the informal—and to the colonial administration unexpected—political alliance between the pastoralists and the farmers in Serengeti, which triggered the first major conflict between local subsistence interests and conservation interests in Serengeti in the mid 1950s, and which ultimately resulted in the partition of the original Serengeti-Ngorongoro reserve into a National Park in the west and a Conservation Area in the east. When the colonial administration prohibited agriculture in Serengeti in 1954 the pastoral Maasai took the side of the farmers and protested against the prohibition. They did so recognizing the importance of agriculture as a risk insurance for the vulnerable pastoral economy, and resenting the restriction on their freedom imposed by the Park authorities. Five years later, in 1959, they only agreed to move from the Western Serengeti on the condition that they would have full rights to live and subsist in the area declared as the Ngorongoro Conservation Area. To the Ngorongoro Maasai this meant the right to continue their pastoral mode of life, but also the possibility of turning to subsistence agriculture in times of need. Thus, when the prohibition on agriculture in the whole of the Ngorongoro Conservation Area finally came in 1975, it was experienced by the pastoralists not only as a further step towards the annihilation of their rights in their homeland, but also as a threat to their existence.

THE FOOD SITUATION

The current food situation of the Ngorongoro Maasai must be seen against this background: the decline of the pastoral economy and the lack of alternative means of subsistence. Though the Ngorongoro Maasai still highly value a purely pastoral diet, they are becoming increasingly dependent on agricultural foods. Maize porridge—a mixture of maize flour, milk and water—is today the dry season staple. This section provides a detailed picture of the food situation among the Ngorongoro Maasai, based on a survey of 10 pastoral households in three different localities during the dry season 1981 (see Århem, 1981 b).[17]

The basic dry season diet consisted of milk, maize porridge and meat. Apart from maize, no other grain was consumed; no rice and no vegetables. Wild plant foods were only collected and eaten occasionally by herd boys and girls when out herding. The average daily milk intake per adult equivalent (AE) ranged between 437–1 466 g in the different settlements with an average of 809 g/AE (see note 18 below for a definition of "adult equivalents"). The daily intake of grain (maize flour) per adult equivalent in the different settlements ranged between 138–389 g with an average of 292 g/AE. There was an inverse relationship between the intake of milk and the intake of grain in the settlement, so that the higher the milk intake, the lower the intake of grain. Milk yields and milk consumption varied considerably from house to house within and between settlements, implying that some houses were more, others less, dependent on grain as a supplementary food. Meat was eaten on an occasional basis, but when eaten, fairly large quantities were consumed. Converted into energy and protein, the data on food consumption showed an average energy intake of 1 874 Cal/AE and day, ranging between 1 651–2 038 Cal/AE and day in the different settlements. The average protein intake in the three settlements varied between 42–53 g reference protein/AE and day, with an average of 48 g/AE and day.

The wide variation in food intake between households and settlements depends on ecological and economic circumstances. Milk yields were highest in areas of favourable range conditions and where water was plentiful, and lowest in areas of poor range conditions and water scarcity. But there were no simple, direct correlations between the level of milk consumption (per capita) and milk yields; this relationship was mediated by economic circumstances, principally the cattle per capita ratio in the different settlements. Thus the locality with poorest range conditions in the sample, but with a relatively high cattle per capita ratio in the settlement (low population density—large herds and few people) had considerably higher levels

71

of milk consumption per capita than the locality in the intermediary zone, characterized by better range conditions, but with a markedly lower cattle per capita ratio in the settlement (high population density—fairly large herds but many people dependent on them).

The fact that the consumption of grain—and meat—was inversely related to the consumption of milk meant that the overall nutritional value of food was highest neither in the settlement of highest average milk yield, nor in the settlement of highest grain consumption, but in the settlement, situated on the dry plain, where the diet was most balanced in terms of the consumption of milk and grain. In other words, the most adequate diet combined milk and meat on the one hand, and grain on the other, in fairly balanced proportions. Where either milk or grain dominated, the nutritional standard was lower. The households displaying the most adequate food standards were those with the highest cattle per capita ratio, that is, those with sufficiently large herds to maintain both a high milk yield and an adequate level of commercial offtake from livestock sales for the purchase of grain. Food standards were thus highest when and where the pastoral prosperity—as measured by the cattle per capita ratio—was successfully converted into both milk and grain in balanced proportions.

A measure of the general importance of grain in the pastoral diet was obtained by determining the relative contribution of milk, grain and meat to the energy and protein intake in the sample households. The study indicated that grain on the average provided 53 % of the total household energy intake while milk and meat together provided 44 % of the energy intake. The remaining 3 % was accounted for by other foods, mainly honey (in honey beer) and sugar (in tea). Milk and meat contributed 72 % and grain 28 % of the household protein intake.

The basic diet varied considerably according to the age and sex of the consumer. Men drank fresh milk more often than they ate grain or meat, while women and children ate maize porridge much more frequently than they drank fresh milk or ate meat. Thus men conformed to the ideal pastoral diet to a greater extent than did women and children, who relied rather more heavily on grain. Though exact comparative measurements were lacking, it is clear that men consumed considerably more milk than women and children (Århem, 1981 b).

Food consumption profiles for males and females of different age groups suggest, on the other hand, that the diet of women and children was more nutritiously "efficient" than that of the men: the energy value of each 100 g food consumed was highest among adult women and lowest among adult or old men. Similarly, the gross protein value per 100 g food was highest among women, but lowest

72

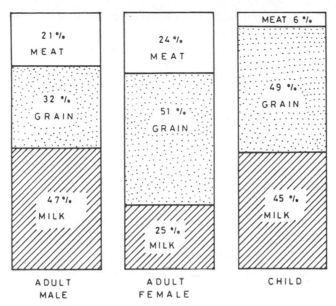

21 % MEAT	24 % MEAT	MEAT 6 %
32 % GRAIN	51 % GRAIN	49 % GRAIN
47 % MILK	25 % MILK	45 % MILK
ADULT MALE	ADULT FEMALE	CHILD

Fig. 5. Food consumption profiles. Relative frequency of consumption of different foods according to age and sex of consumer, expressed as percentage of total mandays of consumption for each consumer category (cf. Table 8).

among (weaned) children (Fig 5; Table 8). This is due to the fact that maize flour is richer both in energy and protein per weight unit than the other kind of foods consumed.

A tentative calculation of food adequacy on the basis of the data on actual food intake per household shows on the one hand that there was a notable energy deficiency in the dry season pastoral diet, and on the other that there was an equally significant protein surplus in the diet. On the whole, the dry season diet in the pastoral household satisfied 67 % of the estimated household energy requirements, while

Table 8. *Food consumption profiles: Dry season nutritional values per 100 g food*

	Energy (Cal)	Protein (g reference protein)
Adult Male Profile	208	7
Adult Female Profile	268	8
Child Profile	226	5

Compare Fig. 5, and Århem, 1981 *b*: Appendix 4.

73

the protein requirements were met in all households with an overall adequacy of 141% (Århem, 1981 b).[18]

Shifting the focus from the household and settlement level to the community level (Ngorongoro as a whole), two basic factors concerning the pastoral food situation in Ngorongoro emerge. First, an estimate of the total, annual community food yield from pastoral herds —milk, meat and blood—revealed that the pastoral foods were able to satisfy only some 60% of the estimated community energy requirements for the year 1980. This estimate takes account of seasonal variations in pastoral food yields and their nutritional value. There was, in other words, a demand for supplementary food sources—that is, grain—corresponding to about 40% of the total community energy needs. Secondly, a survey of the total community supply of grain for the same period—that is, grain available for purchase by the pastoral community—showed that the supply fell far short of the demand. During the period August 1980 to July 1981, when records were available, the supply of grain in the Ngorongoro Conservation Area satisfied—at the most—some 85% of the community demand (Århem, 1981 b).

The official body responsible for providing and distributing grain and other consumer goods to the shops in the area, the Regional Trading Corporation (RTC), provides only a small fraction of the total supply of grain available. The study in 1981 showed that on the whole only 15% of the total supply in the Conservation Area was provided by the RTC, while the remaining 85% was obtained by private shopkeepers and traders, or by the pastoralists themselves, directly from the producers in neighbouring agricultural areas (Århem, 1981 b).

Summing up, there is currently an evident shortage of food, pastoral as well as agricultural, among the Ngorongoro Maasai. The system of pastoral production is not capable of supporting the pastoral population on a year-round and self-sustaining basis. The pastoralists need grain to supplement their pastoral diet. But there is not enough grain available in the local shops to meet the demand. This shortage of grain is particularly pronounced during the dry season when milk yields are at their lowest.

Though the food situation is critical, there is, however, no evidence of famine or acute starvation at the community level. The food shortage is partial and seasonal: it refers to energy deficiency and is essentially concentrated to the dry season. During the wet season food is usually sufficient and occasionally abundant, thus to some extent making up for the dry season deficiency. It is plausible to assume that the pastoralists are physiologically adapted to this seasonal fluctuation between scarcity and abundance of food (cf. Little,

1980). Medical records from local dispensaries and the hospital in Endulen (see below) report few deficiency-related diseases, and medical personnel in the area stressed that the overall nutritional standard is comparatively better among the pastoralists than among neighbouring cultivators. This is no doubt due to the high protein value of the pastoral diet.

Yet, all evidence suggests that the Ngorongoro Maasai have experienced a decline in food standards over the past two decades. The pastoralists themselves emphatically stressed that the food situation had deteriorated. They see the short supply of grain as the major problem. They also perceive a decline in health standards as a result of the increasing food shortage. The falling cattle per capita ratio and the changing composition of pastoral herds in Ngorongoro lend support to this view.

TRADE AND INCOME: THE TIES TO THE MARKET

The dependence on grain ties the Ngorongoro Maasai to the economy of the wider society. As cultivation is prohibited in Ngorongoro, the pastoralists sell livestock to obtain grain. The subsistence-oriented pastoral economy is turning into an increasingly exchange-oriented, partly commercialized livestock economy. Grain is purchased in local village shops; only when it is not available in the local shops do the pastoralists go outside the Conservation Area to look for grain—to Piaya, Malambo, Loliondo and Karatu. Consequently, there is among the Ngorongoro Maasai a very real need for cash; cash for purchasing not only grain, but also cloth, school uniforms, sugar, tea and durable consumer goods like pots, containers and the like.

The major trading centres in the Ngorongoro Conservation Area are Endulen, Nainokanoka and Olairobi. Their history as trading centres goes back long before the villagization campaign; they were well established already in the early 1940s. In each of these villages there were at the time of the village survey in 1980 several private shops, owned and run by non-Maasai traders (usually of Asian or Somali origin), and one cooperative village shop run by the Maasai themselves. In the outlying villages there were only one or two shops, sometimes none at all: in Osinoni there was no shop and in Esere the shop was open only irregularly (cf. Appendix 5). All in all, there were 19 private shops and five cooperative village shops in Ngorongoro in 1980.

The trading villages in Ngorongoro are, however, rather somnolent places, even by regional standards. Commerce appears to have been more lively in the 1950s than today (Jacobs, 1978; Masai-Monduli

Table 9. *Availability of consumer goods in the Ngorongoro Conservation Area: A sample of shops in different villages, September 1980*

	Kakesio	Endulen	Olairobi	Olbalbal	Naino-kanoka	Nairobi
Maize flour	×	×	×	×	×	
Rice	×	×				
Sugar		×				
Salt		×				
Tea		×	×	×		
Milk powder		×	×			
Biscuits			×		×	
Sweets		×	×		×	
Tobacco		×				
Cloth (*shuka*)		×	×	×		×
Shirts/School uniform		×	×	×	×	×
Blankets		×	×			
Metal containers/Pots				×	×	
Plates				×	×	
Torches/Batteries		×				
Pens & paper		×				
Matches	×		×	×	×	×
Toilet soap	×	×	×		×	×
Washing soap					×	×

Source: Own survey 1980.

Distric Book). In 1980 there were very few commodities available in the village shops (see Table 9). The principal commodities were cloth, blankets, matches and soap. Pots and plates were available in a few shops. The only important food available in larger—though insufficient—quantities was maize flour. Rice and sugar were scarce and only occasionally available. Price levels differed between private and cooperative village shops. The goods were more expensive in the private shops. However, the supply of goods was better and the range of goods wider in the private shops, which means that the pastoralists largely depend on the private traders.[19]

There are various reasons for the decline in commerce and trade in Ngorongoro. One is the restrictions on private enterprise imposed by the state. Another is the poor transport facilities in the Conservation Area. The inaccessibility of the outlying villages to some extent explains the poor supplies of commodities in the village shops at present. There are no access roads to the villages of Esere, Osinoni and Kapenjiro, while several other villages are only seasonally accessible by road. The road to the Melenda plateau and the Empakaai highlands, where the majority of the pastoralists in Ngorongoro live, goes through the Ngorongoro Crater. It is in very bad condition, particularly as it ascends the steep slopes of Empakaai. Only the villages of Endulen and Olairobi are relatively easily accessible by road throughout the year (cf. Appendix 5).[20] The distribution of goods in Ngorongoro suffers in consequence. While a lorry can take 150 bags or more of maize flour to Endulen, it cannot take more than 50 bags at a time to Nainokanoka and the other villages in Melenda and Empakaai area due to the bad road. Bus services exist only at the Ngorongoro tourist centre. From here buses travel regularly to Oldeani, Mbulu and Arusha. There are a few privately owned lorries in Endulen and Kakesio. These lorries are occasionally hired by shop keepers in other villages to transport goods in and out of the Ngorongoro Conservation Area.

Not only are there few commodities to buy in Ngorongoro; the sources of cash for the pastoral households are equally few. Wage labour opportunities are few and unattractive to the pastoralists. They consist of sporadic and unskilled jobs such as construction work and road maintenance in the vicinity of the tourist and major trading centres. Only a few pastoralists are engaged in periodic wage labour: in 1980 less than 75 local pastoralists, all men, were engaged in wage labour.

The local and seasonal sale of milk, honey beer and resin (gum arabic) also provide some households with a source of money. These cash earning activities are in the hands of women. Surplus milk is sold during the wet season in the staff village and near the tourist centre in Ngorongoro, and in the trading centres like Endulen and Nainokanoka. Women also prepare a local brand of beer based on honey and sugar. Again, the beer is sold in trading centres where there is a great and constant demand. A considerable amount of honey beer is also consumed out in the pastoral settlements. In parts of the Conservation Area, notably in the Kakesio ward, the collection of resin was until recently an additional, significant source of cash among women. The crude resin was sold to local shops and traders. However, in July 1980 the Conservation Authority prohibited the collection of resin in the area on the grounds that it was against the conservation rules.

Livestock sale, which is entirely in the hands of the men, is by far the most important source of cash in the pastoral household. Livestock is sold throughout the year, when considered necessary by the household head and when marketing opportunities exist. Sales tend, however, to be more frequent during the dry season, when the need for grain is greatest. Both cattle and small stock are sold, the proportions varying from year to year. In the study of 10 pastoral households during the dry season 1981, cattle sales were a considerably

Table 10. *Cattle sales in the Ngorongoro Conservation Area 1961–80: Official marketing figures*

Year	No. of cattle sold	Commercial offtake (% of total cattle herd)
1961	5 468	4.3
1963	4 031	3.4
1965	3 977	3.6[a]
1976	807	0.7[a]
1978	510	0.5
1980	924[b]	0.8

[a] This figure is based on an estimate of the total cattle herd in the Ngorongoro Conservation Area (cf. Fig. 2 and Århem 1981 *a*).

[b] Estimate for the whole year based on sales figures from the first 8 months of the year.

Sources: Official statistics from NCAA and TLMC.

more important source of cash than the sale of small stock (Århem, 1981 *b*). Steers and bulls are sold in preference to cows and heifers. Official market prices are state-controlled and tend to be unelastic, while unofficial market prices vary considerably from year to year, even from season to season. In 1980 (January–August) the average official market price was 1 275 Tanzanian Shillings (TShs) per head of cattle and 195 TShs per head of small stock. A follow-up survey in 1981 gave a slightly higher market value for cattle (1 420 TShs) and a lower value for small stock (175 TShs).[21]

The official figures on commercial offtake from cattle sales in Ngorongoro show a drastic decline over the past two decades—from 3–4% in the early 1960s to 0.5–0.8% in the late 1970s (Table 10).[22] These figures conceal the fact that large numbers of livestock are sold outside the official marketing institutions. There are indications that the unofficial marketing of livestock has increased during the past decade. The detailed study of 10 households in 1981 revealed that, in fact, the overhelming majority of livestock sales currently takes place outside the official marketing channels. In the sample, 87% of the animals sold were sold locally to private livestock traders or local herd owners. Thus, only 13% of the animals were sold through the official marketing channels (Århem, 1981 *b*).

The total commercial offtake, including unofficial sales, was in the range of 3–4% of the total cattle herd in the sample. The overall picture emerging from the study is that the majority of pastoral households are subsistence-oriented with a low rate of commercial offtake (ranging between 1–5% in individual households) but that there does exist a small number of households which have a considerably higher rate of commercial offtake (over 10% of the household herd; ibid). This means that, on the whole, the commercial offtake from cattle has remained remarkably constant for at least the past 20 years. Forsbrooke made a survey of commercial offtake from cattle sales in Ngorongoro during the years 1961–63, which showed an average annual offtake rate of 4% of the total cattle herd (reported in Dirschl, 1966). What has changed is the proportion of sales inside and outside the official marketing channels: the volume of unofficial sales has increased substantially at the expense of official sales. The commercial offtake from small stock sales is much lower, the annual average currently ranging between 1–2% of the small stock herd.

There are several reasons why livestock sales through the official marketing channels have declined in recent years. One important factor is the poor performance of the official marketing institutions. Of three livestock markets until recently operating in the Ngorongoro Conservation Area, only the one in Endulen was operating on a regular basis in 1980–81 (cf. Appendix 5). The high market fees and the fact that buyers are few and rarely absorb the livestock offered at the market also discourage the stock owners from bringing their animals.[23] Put simply, the pastoralists prefer to sell their animals to local traders and stock owners, or to take their animals to Kenya where they get better prices and where more goods are available on the market.

The overall low commercial offtake from livestock sales among the Ngorongoro Maasai is partly a result of their subsistence-oriented economy. Indeed, it could be argued that in a subsistence-oriented and cattle-based pastoral economy the commercial offtake could not be much higher than it is without endangering the reproduction and stability of the domestic herds. Forsbrooke (1964; 1972: 159, 193) has shown that the Ngorongoro Maasai on the average slaughter some 4% of their cattle for home consumption and ritual purposes, and that there is an average loss of about 10% of the total cattle herd from natural causes. These figures compare well with the figures for optimal offtake from pastoral herds under subsistence conditions calculated by Dahl and Hjort (1976: 175). They estimate an optimal offtake of 8% for slaughter and sale, and a typical loss of 8% in natural death, giving a total offtake rate of 16% under optimal pastoral conditions.

In the case of the Ngorongoro Maasai, the low commercial offtake must, however, also be seen in the context of the poor supply of commodities in the outlying pastoral villages. There are very few commodities to buy, and the supply of grain does not meet the demand of the pastoral community. There is an additional fact to be taken into account in this context. The barter terms of trade for the

Table 11. *Barter terms of trade in the Ngorongoro Conservation Area, 1961–81*

	Amount of maize flour obtained for one head of cattle					
	1961	1965	1977	1978	1980	1981
Maize flour (kg)	164[a]	200[a]	338[a]	600[a]	464[b]	406[b]

[a] Figures calculated from Tanzanian Household Survey, 1969 and TLMC statistics.
[b] Based on own surveys 1980–81.

two principal commodities involved—cattle and maize flour—have, over the past two decades, developed in favor of the pastoralists in Ngorongoro. For one head of cattle sold in 1980 the seller received more than twice the amount of maize flour he received in the early 1960s. This means that the cattle owner needs to sell less than half as many cattle to obtain the same amount of grain as twenty years ago (Table 11). Yet, it must be borne in mind that during the same period the demand for grain has increased substantially due to the falling cattle per capita ratio.

At the present levels of commercial offtake from livestock sales (set at 4% of the cattle herd and 1.5% of the small stock herd; Table 12) the pastoral economy of the Ngorongoro Maasai generates an average annual per capita income of 441 TShs (including income from both cattle and small stock sales) at 1980 price levels. If an estimated 70% of the income is spent on the purchase of grain (a reasonable assumption) the pastoral economy has at present a potential capacity to meet

Table 12. *Income terms of trade in the Ngorongoro Conservation Area: Income from cattle sales 1961–1980*

Year	Annual per capita income (TShs)	Purchasing power (kg maize flour/capita)
1961	57[a]	75
1965	74[a]	80
1977	227[b]	90
1978	374[b]	144
1980	412[b]	150

[a] Based on human population estimates (cf. Fig. 2 and Århem 1981 a).
[b] Based on an estimated total commercial offtake of 4% (see text).
Sources: Tanzania Household Survey 1969, TLMC statistics and price figures, and official population statistics from the NCAA.

the total community demand for grain if it were locally available in sufficient quantities. As was shown above, this is, however, not the case. The potential remains unrealized.

Though no information is available on the grain supply in Ngorongoro in the early 1960s, a comparison of the purchasing power of the pastoral community in 1961 and 1980 indicates that it has in fact doubled. The average per capita income in 1980 implied a capacity to buy twice as much maize flour as the per capita income of 1961 (Table 12). However, this fact cannot be taken as an indication of any real improvement in living conditions since it ignores the fact that absolute food yields from livestock have fallen during the same period (because the number of cattle has decreased) and that absolute food requirements—particularly the need for grain—have increased (because the number of people has increased), and that there exists a shortage of grain in the area.

The general conclusion emerging from this discussion is that the inadequate supply of grain at community level is a major constraint in the food system of the Ngorongoro Maasai. The shortage and irregular supply of grain in the village shops, rather than the low rates of commercial offtake from livestock sales, account for the seasonal inadequacies in the pastoral diet. In fact, the poor supply of grain goes a long way to explain the low commercial offtake from livestock sales.

These predicaments of the pastoral economy in Ngorongoro have profound effects on the situation of the women in the pastoral households. Livestock sales are, as noted above, entirely in the hands of men. Even if women are allocated a small herd at marriage to keep in trust for their male children, it is only men who own animals, and it is only men who have the right to dispose of animals in livestock sales. In light of this, the other sources of cash in the pastoral household—the sale of milk, honey beer and resin—become important, because they are basically controlled by women. In fact, they are the only sources of cash for women.

In the traditional division of labour it is women who are directly responsible for feeding the pastoral family. As wife and mother, the woman milks the cows and decides about the distribution of milk among the family members. Today she is also largely responsible for obtaining maize flour from village shops. But she does not control the money for which she must buy the grain. She receives money from her husband, brother or father. Yet, it is her task to see that the money suffices to buy enough grain for the family. This is why women are eager to obtain their own cash through selling milk, beer and resin. They know what the family needs, but often the money they receive from their menfolk is not enough to cover the needs, particularly under current economic circumstances when the pastoral household is becoming increasingly dependent on grain.

There is a further distressing implication of this situation. In her role as provider of food, the mother and wife is the last to get a share of the available food in the house. It is her responsibility to see that the rest of the family is fed, and if food is scarce she is the one who gets the least.

RESOURCE DEVELOPMENT

Water supply

Life in Maasailand is profoundly conditioned by the irregular rainfall pattern and the seasonal scarcity of surface water. During the rains —usually coming in a few, heavy showers between November and April—seasonal rivers, pools and springs supply the whole Conservation Area with sufficient water for people and livestock. In the dry season, however, water is scarce in most parts. Streams and pools in the lowlands dry up and people and livestock congregate around the permanent streams in the highlands and near the few and scattered springs, wells and artificial water points. In the lowland villages of Kakesio, Osinoni, and Esere the pastoralists rely almost entirely on water from a spring in Esere and wells in the dry bed of the Kakesio River. The highland villages rely largely on permanent streams or water piped from the streams to a few communal taps at the village centres. Piped water for domestic use is available in six of the nine registered villages in Ngorongoro. Yet in all villages natural water sources and traditional wells play an important role in the domestic water supply. Given the wide distribution of the pastoral population, many settlements are very far from the communal taps and therefore make little use of them (Table 13; cf. Map 5).

Similarly, most of the pastoral villages rely heavily on natural or traditional water points for their range water supply during the dry season: wells, troughs and ditches are dug in the dry stream beds or constructed near natural springs. Six of the villages have access to piped range water. Again, outlying pastoral settlements have to trek their livestock long distances every other or third day during the dry season in order to reach these water points. Only in one village, Osinoni, is there a functioning large dam, and it serves the entire Kakesio ward (Table 13).

The heavy reliance on natural and traditional water sources conceals the fact that efforts have been made over the past two decades to improve the water supply situation in Ngorongoro. A number of

Table 13. *Distribution of major water sources in the Ngorongoro Conservation Area (in use, August 1980)*

	Kakesio	Osinoni	Esere	Endulen	Olairobi	Olbalbal, Oldoinyo Oogol	Nainokanoka, Ilkeepusi	Alaililai	Nairobi
Domestic Water									
Permanent streams or natural springs			×	×		(×)	×		×
Traditional wells	(×)	×			(×)	(×)	(×)		(×)
Piped water				×	(×)	(×)	×	×	×
Range Water									
Permanent streams or natural springs			×	×			×		×
Traditional wells or small dams	(×)					(×)	(×)		(×)
Piped water and trough				×	(×)	(×)	×	×	×
Large dams		×							

× Present in the village and considered adequate.
(×) Present in the village but not considered adequate, or used mainly by peripheral settlements.
Source: Own survey 1980.

pipes, dams, troughs and hafirs have been constructed—most of them in compensation for the water sources lost in Serengeti at the creation of the National Park—but are today broken down or otherwise out of order. The two boreholes and pumps at Lemuta and Ndjureta in the Oogol hills (constructed in 1959–60) used to provide critical dry season water to the settlements in the area but were out of order—and had been so intermittently for many years—at the time of the survey in 1980. Two dams and a hafir in the Kakesio-Endulen area, also constructed in 1959, were breached already in the early 1960s and have since then been defunct. In Alaililai village on the Melenda plateau a gravity pipe from the Munge River of the Olmoti highland (constructed in 1941) used to pipe water to seven different water points, only one of which is functioning today. The overall result of this situation is that the pastoralists remain dependent, perhaps increasingly so, on the scarce natural water sources and their traditional means of exploiting them.

In spite of the failures in developing the water supplies in Ngorongoro, the pastoralists consider the general water situation adequate in all but two of the registered villages—Olairobi and Olbalbal, both with access to piped water. The reason water supplies were not considered adequate in these two villages was said to be the considerable increase in their population over the past two decades. Both villages are comparatively large, and rely to a great extent on traditional wells in the dry season. Many settlements are located very far from the principal water sources in the villages; some as far as 10–15 km away from the village centre.

Livestock health and veterinary services

Along with the scarcity of surface water, the presence of livestock diseases is a basic environmental constraint in Ngorongoro, profoundly influencing the living conditions of its pastoral inhabitants. A whole range of livestock diseases are endemic in Ngorongoro, presenting a serious obstacle to livestock management. On the whole, livestock diseases—particularly tick-borne diseases like east coast fever—are a greater problem in the moister highlands than on the dry plains. Calf mortality is consequently higher in the highlands than on the plains (Homewood and Rodgers, 1984).[24] The Ngorongoro Maasai consider east coast fever, foot and mouth disease and anthrax the most serious and widespread diseases in the area. Trypanosomiasis is essentially confined to the dense woodlands, while malignant catarrhal fever, transmitted by wildebeest, is confined in time and space to the calving period of the wildebeest and the migration routes on the open plain (see Chapter Four above and Table 14).

According to the pastoralists, east coast fever was on the increase at the time of the survey (1980). In all the villages except Kakesio and Endulen the pastoralists claimed that livestock health had declined during the past two decades. In the lowland villages of Esere and Olbalbal the alleged decline in livestock health was said to be due to the spread of east coast fever and malignant catarrhal fever, while in the villages of the central and eastern highlands the decline was blamed on insufficient grazing land and poor grasses. This, in turn, was said to be the result of the strict conservation measures in the area—the ban on grass burning and the exclusion of the pastoralists and their herds from traditionally utilized pastures, water sources and salt licks (cf. Chapter Three). In Kakesio, on the other hand, livestock health was said to have improved as a result of decreasing grazing pressure: many pastoralists have left the area after intensified hostilities with the neighbouring Sukuma people. In Endulen the condition of livestock was said to be stable for similar reasons.[25]

Veterinary services are rudimentary in Ngorongoro. Veterinary assistants are stationed in two villages, Endulen and Nainokanoka,

Table 14. *Distribution of livestock diseases in the Ngorongoro Conservation Area: The view of the pastoralists*

	Kakesio	Esere	Endulen	Olairobi	Olbalbal	Nainokanoka	Alalilai	Nairobi
East Coast Fever	×	×	×	×	×	×	×	×
Foot and Mouth Disease	(×)	×	×	×	×	(×)	×	×
Anthrax	(×)		×	×	(×)	×	×	×
Nairobi Sheep Disease	×	(×)	×			×	×	×
Black-water					×	×	×	×
Trypanosomiasis	×	×	×					
Lipis (unidentified)						×	×	×
Brucellosis					×		×	
Malignant Catarrhal Fever (Snotsiekte)		(×)			×			
Anaplasmosis	×					×		

× Experienced as a major livestock health problem in the village (own survey, 1980).
(×) Reported as present in the village (The Arusha RIDEP Village Profile Survey, 1979) but not experienced as a major problem (own survey 1980).

and there is a veterinary centre at the headquarters of the Ngorongoro Conservation Area Authority, which is intended to serve the whole Conservation Area. Drugs and appropriate equipment are in scarce supply. The pastoralists often have to go to Arusha to obtain drugs. There are dips in seven of the nine villages, but most of them are intermittently out of order due to the scarce and irregular supply of acaricides (cf. Appendix 5).

It is possible that the high incidence of east coast fever in Ngorongoro is, in fact, related to the poor operation and irregular use of dips in the area. Tick borne diseases like east coast fever can normally be controlled by regular dipping. However, irregular dipping can have the contrary effect: the natural resistance of the sturdy local livestock is reduced at the same time as dipping gives insufficient protection from the disease. The unhygienic condition of many dips also enhances the risk of disease transmission. Scarcity of water, mechanical faults in the pump supplying the dip with clean water or lack of fuel for the pump result in dirty water or put the dip entirely out of operation. Willingness to use the dips was never lacking among the pastoralists. On the contrary, the introduction of dipping facilities was met with enthusiasm. However, for the reasons mentioned, the enthusiasm gradually gave way to despondency.[26] Another important

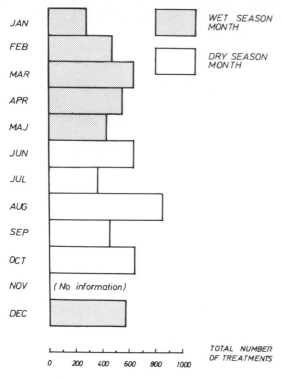

JAN

FEB

MAR

APR

MAJ

JUN

JUL

AUG

SEP

OCT

NOV (No information)

DEC

WET SEASON
MONTH

DRY SEASON
MONTH

TOTAL NUMBER
OF TREATMENTS

0   200   400   600   800   1000

Fig. 6. Seasonal incidence of principal diseases: Total number of cases of treatment per month at Endulen hospital, 1980.

reason for the irregular dipping in Ngorongoro is the long distances herders have to trek their animals between settlement and dip. With the present distribution of dips, and given the transhumant system of land use, herders could hardly dip their animals as often as required; in fact, even if the dips worked and acaricides were regularly available it would imply an extremely heavy work load for them.

HEALTH

The health situation among the Ngorongoro Maasai appears in many respects typical of East African pastoralists in general, living in a semi-arid environment where water is seasonally scarce and health services rudimentary. An examination of monthly treatment records from the Endulen hospital for a one-year period (1980) reveals that respiratory diseases (including pneumonia and bronchitis), eye diseases (trachoma, conjunctivitis), diarrhoea and venereal diseases were most commonly treated (Fig. 6). Tuberculosis was relatively rarely treated but appears to be widespread in the area (cf. Table 15).

86

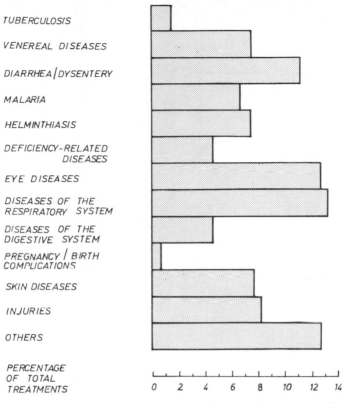

TUBERCULOSIS

VENEREAL DISEASES

DIARRHEA/DYSENTERY

MALARIA

HELMINTHIASIS

DEFICIENCY-RELATED
DISEASES

EYE DISEASES

DISEASES OF THE
RESPIRATORY SYSTEM

DISEASES OF THE
DIGESTIVE SYSTEM

PREGNANCY / BIRTH
COMPLICATIONS

SKIN DISEASES

INJURIES

OTHERS

PERCENTAGE
OF TOTAL
TREATMENTS

0   2   4   6   8   10   12   14

Fig. 7. Relative incidence of principal diseases: Percentage of total number of cases of treatment at Endulen hospital, 1980.

There is a notably low incidence of deficiency-related diseases, which is conspicuous in light of the dry season food shortage documented above. It should be borne in mind, however, that the treatment records give only a very approximate picture of the health situation. They reflect the scarce and irregular supply of drugs in the hospital as much as the incidence of diseases in the area (Fig. 7).

The treament records show that, of the most common diseases, diarrhoea, helminthiasis and eye diseases predominantly affect the young children. Venereal diseases, expectedly, affect essentially the adult population, including a significant proportion of school-age girls, while deficiency-related diseases are more common among children than among adults. Among the adults treated for deficiency-related diseases, the majority were women (Fig. 8).

A comparative note may be of interest here. In a health survey among pastoralists in Uganda, it was found that the most common diseases among children were skin diseases (scabies, tropical ulcer), intestinal and blood parasites (45–80% of the children had malaria

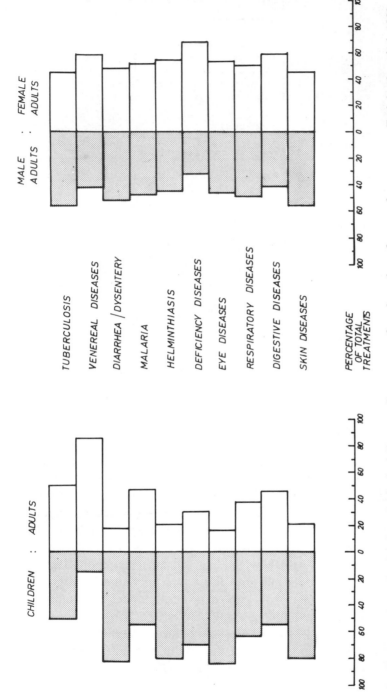

Fig. 8. Age and sex distribution of principal diseases: Percentage of total number of cases of treatment at Endulen hospital, 1980.

Table 15. *Distribution of diseases in the Ngorongoro Conservation Area: The view of the pastoralists*

	Kakesio	Esere	Endulen	Olairobi	Olbalbal	Nainokanoka	Alaililai	Nairobi
Venereal diseases	×	×	×	×	×	×	×	×
Tuberculosis	×	×	×	×		×	×	×
Conjunctivitis/Trachoma	×	×	(×)			×	×	×
Pneumonia	×	×	×			×		×
Malaria	×	×	(×)		×			
Anthrax	×	×			×	(×)		

× Experienced as a major health problem in the village (own survey 1980).
(×) Reported as present in the village (Treatment Records, the Arusha RIDEP Village Profile Survey, 1979) but not experienced as a major health problem (own survey, 1980).

parasites) and eye diseases (25% possibly associated with early trachoma). Protein-calorie malnutrition was very rare (Little, 1980: 482).[27]

The pastoralists' own perceptions of the major health problems complement the picture based on the treatment records. A survey (1980) covering all the pastoral villages in Ngorongoro showed that the pastoralists considered venereal diseases, tuberculosis, eye diseases and pneumonia their most serious health problems. Malaria was seen as a problem only in the lowland villages (Table 15).

The relatively high incidence of eye- and skin diseases is closely related to the predicaments of the pastoral economy and environment: the scarcity of water, the intimate relationship between people and cattle and the consequent abundant presence of germ-carrying flies. Tuberculosis is associated with the milieu in a similar manner; it is transmitted through infected milk, and from person to person in the confined living space of the pastoral settlement. The frequent occurrence of venereal diseases reflects two further facts of the Maasai social reality: first, that there is a considerable interaction between the local rural society and the urban and semi-urban centres outside Ngorongoro; and secondly, that there is a high degree of sexual freedom in Maasai society. According to Maasai custom an unmarried and uncircumcised girl is free to have sexual relations with practically any circumcised man outside her own and her mother's clan (or sub-clan), and a married man is expected to give his fellow clansmen and age mates sexual access to his wives.

Health services in the Ngorongoro Conservation Area suffer the same limitations as in other marginal, rural areas in Tanzania. Drugs and equipment are in short supply, hygienic conditions in dispensaries are deficient and the health personnel is often poorly motivated. There is one hospital (in Endulen) and four government dispensaries (in Kakesio, Endulen, Nainokanoka and at the headquarters of the Ngorongoro Conservation Area Authority). The hospital was built in 1976 and is run by an Austrian-based mission society. It is specialized in the treatment of tuberculosis but provides general medical services, including minor surgery. Until 1981 it ran a mobile health service covering the entire Conservation Area. The dispensaries are manned by a medical assistant, a rural medical aid, or nurse, all generally of non-Maasai origin.[28]

The pastoralists in each village were asked if, in their opinion, the general health situation had changed over the past two decades. In every village the response was emphatically the same: people were healthier 20 years ago. The reason given was that the food situation had since then deteriorated. Today people have less milk and less grain than before, when herds were bigger and cultivation was permitted in Ngorongoro.

Summing up, the current health situation of the Ngorongoro Maasai must be seen in the light of, on the one hand, the deterioration of their food situation, and on the other, the deficient health services in the area. In the entire Eastern Zone, for example, there is only one dispensary staffed by a single medical assistant and serving a population of some 6 800 people. The bulk of the pastoral population live far from the dispensary—the people in Nairobi and Kapenjiro have to walk some 30–40 km to reach it. Knowing that the supplies of drugs usually are in short supply and that the medical assistant is only periodically present—ostensibly due to the shortage of drugs—the villagers, who have no other means of transport than walking, rarely find the trip worthwhile.

EDUCATION

There are primary schools in all villages in the Ngorongoro Conservation Area. Standards 1–3 (Universal Primary Education) are offered in all schools, while Standards 4–7 are offered in only four villages (Endulen, Kakesio, Nainokanoka and Olairobi). The schools in Endulen, Kakesio and Nainokanoka have boarding facilities for children living far away from the school. In September 1980 there were 54 boarded students in Nainokanoka and 68 in Endulen. While staffing seemed adequate in the schools in the larger trading centres, the

90

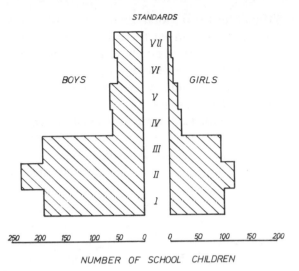

Fig. 9. School attendance in the Ngorongoro Conservation Area, 1980: Sex distribution from Standard 1–7.

smaller schools in the more remote villages like Esere, Osinoni, Olbalbal and Nairobi were understaffed; when, for example, the single teacher or teaching assistant was ill or absent, teaching came to a standstill.

School attendance is low among the pastoralists in Ngorongoro. Only about 40–45% of the total school-age population (7–13 years of age) actually attend school regularly. The enrollment rate is higher, somewhere between 65–75% of the total school-age population in the area (Appendices 3 and 4). This figure compares well with the regional average. Attendance is markedly higher among boys than among girls, and the ratio of boys to girls attending school increases in the higher classes. In Standards 1–3 about 65% of the students are boys, while in Standard 7 the proportion of boys is 95% of all students. Of the students finishing Standard 3 only about 30% continue to Standard 4 (Fig. 9; cf. Appendices 3 and 4).

The reasons behind the poor school attendance are many. Two major factors can be isolated: the first has to do with the nature of the pastoral economy, and the second with the position of women in Maasai society. The pastoral household is dependent on young boys (and girls) for daily herding labour; it is the young boys who perform most of the herding routines. The process of learning the herding duties and proper livestock management is long, and boys are therefore given herding responsibilities early in life. In the traditional division of labour—still very much in force among the Ngorongoro Maasai—the young men (*ilmuran*) are essentially freed from routine herding. It is therefore difficult for the pastoral household to dispense with the labour of the young boys. Indeed there is often a labour shortage in the household, forcing girls or adults to help in herding. Under these circumstances only large households with many children can send children to school; usually one or two boys are sent to school while the rest remain in the household.

The extremely poor school attendance among girls must be seen in relation to the fact that women in general occupy a subordinate position in the authority structure of Maasai society. Men are in control of local political affairs and men communicate and interact with society at large. Women are expected to attend to household duties and to bring up the young children. They are confined to the domestic sphere. Thus, while the elders can see the importance of boys attending school, they see no reason to send girls to school. Moreover, as girls marry very young in Maasai society, they are early absorbed in household duties.

An additional problem in this context is the wide dispersion and relative mobility of the pastoral settlements. With the present distribution of schools in the area, many children have a very long way to walk to school. In view of the abundant wildlife—including dangerous beasts like buffalos, elephants and lions—this is particularly unsatisfactory. There are boarding schools in each ward for the children living in outlying areas, but the boarding school is not an attractive option for the pastoralists. The milieu at the boarding school is totally unfamiliar to the children, the food is different and often of poorer quality than the food at home. The child is surrounded by strangers, and in the highlands the sleeping quarters are often freezing cold during the nights.

SUMMARY

The distribution of infrastructural services in the Conservation Area is uneven and generally unsatisfactory, both in an objective sense and in the eyes of the local pastoralists (see Appendices 5 and 6). Efforts have been made, particularly during the villagization campaign in the mid-1970s, to improve the situation, but the results have been poor. Transport and communication services remain poorly developed, roads are bad and insufficiently maintained. Medical and veterinary services are irregular and inadequate. Livestock marketing facilities are seriously deficient. Primary educational institutions are relatively better developed but suffer a number of constraints: teachers and schools are few for the vast area to be served and the school system is ill adapted to the pastoral social and economic reality. The supply and distribution of essential commodities, including basic foods—particularly grain—is grossly inadequate. All in all, Ngorongoro is marginal in terms of infrastructural and basic socioeconomic services.

The food situation has deteriorated over the past two decades; the pastoral household owns less cattle and consequently has less milk than before. The Maasai associate this deterioration of the food situation with what they experience as a decline in health, implying a falling standard of living. People are becoming increasingly dependent on the external market over which they have little or no control; they have to sell livestock in order to purchase grain. Economic differentiation among the pastoralists is increasing; the gap between rich and poor is widening.

The system of pastoral production in Ngorongoro is at present not capable of supporting the pastoral population on a self-sustaining basis. In order to meet the community demand for food, grain has to be injected into the system. The pastoral community depends on the import of grain. The total supply of grain in the Conservation Area is however insufficient to satisfy this demand. The problem is aggravated by the ban on agriculture in the area. There is, in other words, a shortage of grain at the community level. This shortage is particularly pronounced during the dry season, when pastoral food yields are at their lowest.

A study of food intake at the household level revealed a dry season energy deficiency in the pastoral households; energy needs are satisfied only to some 65–75%. During the wet season, however, it appears that the pastoral diet is adequate. Protein needs are well satisfied during both seasons; there is indeed a considerable protein surplus in the pastoral diet. This probably accounts for an apparently adequate overall nutritional standard among the pastoralists; though the pastoralists themselves experience a decline in food standards and see food shortage as a major problem, there appear to be few deficiency-related diseases among them.

6. Conflicting Views on Development and Conservation in Ngorongoro

This Chapter shifts the focus from the material conditions of life, described in the previous Chapter, to the pastoralists' own perception of their situation. On the basis of interviews and group discussions with pastoralists in different parts of the Conservation Area it describes what they see as the main problems of community development and how they define their relationship with the authorities which most influence their lives.

The problem experienced as most critical was the dry season food shortage. The pastoralists see a decline in the size of family herds and the prohibition of agriculture as the main causes of the food shortage. The situation is aggravated by the scarce and irregular supply of grain in the village shops. The deterioration of the food situation is, in turn, seen as responsible for a decline in health standards. The pastoralists are of the opinion that the solution to this problem is to lift the ban on cultivation in the Conservation Area. They see, in other words, subsistence cultivation in conjunction with pastoralism as the only way to obtain self-sufficiency in terms of food supply.

The second major problem in the eyes of the pastoralists was the loss of autonomy brought about by the conservation rules and restrictions. The restrictions set artificial limits to resource utilization, limits which the pastoralists see as unwarranted. At present, when the livestock density in the highlands is high and pressures on resources relatively heavy, the fact that the pastoralists are deprived of valuable traditional grazing land is felt particularly strongly and experienced as having detrimental effects on human and livestock health. There is less grass for the animals and less milk for the people.

Other general problems experienced as obstacles to community development were the poor communications and the inadequate health and veterinary services. Water scarcity and cattle theft were seen as problems in particular villages. Schools were considered adequate in all villages, possibly reflecting the fairly cool interest among the Maasai elders in their children's schooling. The poor livestock marketing facilities were mentioned as a problem only in one village. Again this may indicate little interest in the commercialization of the pastoral economy, but it also underscores the fact that the pastoralists see the short supply of grain as the most serious problem. The indifference to the problem of livestock marketing must furthermore be seen in the context of two additional features of the current pastoral reality in Ngorongoro: the declining family herds and the numerous opportunities for selling livestock outside the official marketing channels. All in all, subsistence cultivation as a supplement to pastoral economic activities, rather than an increased commercialization of the pastoral economy, is seen as the only solution to their basic problem of dry season food shortage (cf. Appendix 6).

These views to a large extent define the pastoralists' attitude towards the Conservation Authority. The relationship between the pastoralists and the Authority is characterized by a great deal of antagonism. The pastoralists express resentment towards the Conservation Authority, while the Authority and its officials see the pastoralists as an obstacle to, and a problem in the task of managing the natural resources of the area.

THE VIEW OF THE PASTORALISTS

The pastoralists feel subject to too many rules and restrictions imposed upon them by the Authority. They are forbidden to cultivate, and in some parts of the Conservation Area they are not allowed to graze their cattle on lands which they used in the past. They arc excluded from the use of certain water sources and salt licks, they have been evicted from the Western Serengeti and the Ngorongoro Crater, and they are no longer allowed to collect resin in the forests, nor to use fire as a means of pasture management to the extent they would like to. All this makes the pastoralists feel inhibited, constrained and unfree. As one elder put it: "We feel like we were confined to the floor of a deep crater, surrounded by steep walls and unable to go where we want or to take our cattle where there is good grass and water."

They know that they are considered an obstacle by the Authority. They are aware of the fact that the primary interest and concern of the Authority is the protection of the wildlife. People and their herds are not allowed to move freely, they say, but the wild animals are. The wildebeest has multiplied over the past few years and taken over former Maasai wet season pastures and driven the domestic herds up into the hills and highlands. Predators roam unmolested and occasionally kill domestic stock. The herd owners are not compensated. The fact that the Authority excludes the pastoralists from grazing land and water sources, and restricts their movement and settlement in the name of wildlife conservation, makes the pastoralists bitter as they know that, by their very presence and long and successful coexistence with the wildlife, they have indeed helped to preserve the natural heritage of the area.

Added to this bitterness is the living memory of the eviction from the pastures and permanent water sources in the Western Serengeti. In 1959 the Maasai were promised full rights to live and subsist in the Ngorongoro Conservation Area. Since then, their rights have been further circumscribed. Today their very presence in Ngorongoro is threatened, and they know it. They also know that their current situation is directly related to their lack of access to the decision-making body of the Authority. The Authority decides their future above their heads. They feel powerless and overruled. The Ngorongoro Maasai say that the national policy of socialism and self-reliance is only for the people in towns and the cultivating peasants living in villages; it does not apply to them, the pastoralists.

All this adds up to a widespread, negative attitude among the pastoralists towards the Conservation Authority. At the same time, the Ngorongoro Maasai express a very strong wish and determination to stay in the area. They are firmly rooted in Ngorongoro, they feel a deep attachment to the land which they have inhabited for generations and which they consider their own: "This is our homeland", they say, "this is where we belong. No matter what happens, even if nothing changes for the better, whether we are allowed to cultivate or not and even if we have to starve and suffer, this is where we want to stay".

THE VIEW OF THE CONSERVATION AUTHORITY

The officials of the Conservation Authority have an entirely different view of the major problems in Ngorongoro. Pastoral land use and the development of the livestock economy are considered incompatible with the conservation of the environment and the development of tourism—the two priority tasks of the current management. Consequently the Authority sees the people and their livestock as an obstacle to the management of the natural resources and a threat to the environment of the area. Current management practices rest on the assumption that the pastoral population and the herds of domestic stock in Ngorongoro are approaching, and locally surpassing, the carrying capacity of the land in an irreversible process of environmental destruction.

It is furthermore assumed that the demand for modern housing and improved social services—seen as inevitable consequences of modernization—will turn the natural environment into an essentially man-made, artificial environment. The present Conservator has publicly expressed his conviction that the current system of extensive, pastoral land use must, in the near future, turn into an intensive system of beef ranching in response to, as it were, the pastoralists' own demand for modernization (Saibull, 1978).

The same view appears in a different version, phrased in the language of political rhetoric: As an outcome of historical circumstances, the Ngorongoro pastoralists find themselves subject to a series of rules and regulations which do not apply to people outside the area. These rules and restrictions are based on legislation which the Conservation Authority regards as definite. It is the Conservation Authority that controls the land and defines its uses within the boundaries of the Conservation Area. Hence, it is argued, the Ngorongoro Maasai do not have the same freedom, rights to and opportunities of self-reliant development as do villagers outside the area. In order to achieve this freedom, which the pastoralists themselves desire, they should be "encouraged" to resettle outside the area.

A CRITICAL COMMENT

In the light of the history of Maasailand and our knowledge of the fate of East African pastoralists in general, this view appears ill-informed if not cynical. Development policies in Tanzania—and livestock policies in particular—have consistently denied pastoral communities the right of self-reliant development, and ranching has tended to replace rather than develop pastoral economies, resulting in increasing subsistence stress and impoverishment among the pastoralists.

In its zeal to achieve the conservation goals, laid down by the 1975 Ngorongoro Conservation Area Ordinance, the Authority has failed in its responsibility to safeguard and promote the interests of the pastoral inhabitants of the area, which was stipulated as another, equally fundamental objective of the Conservation Ordinance (see Chapter Three above). What is more, the Conservation Authority seems little aware of the fact that the Authority itself has contributed to create the predicament in which the pastoralists find themselves, and the problems which both pastoralists and the Authority face today. And the solution to the crisis endorsed by the Authority—to resettle the pastoralists elsewhere—ignores the wishes and strong determination of the Ngorongoro Maasai to remain in the area, and rejects the very policy of multiple land use underlying the creation of the Ngorongoro Conservation Area in 1959.[29]

Moreover, the view held by the Conservation Authority that the pastoralists present an imminent threat to the natural environment in the area is not supported by the facts at hand. It disregards the fact that the environment of the Serengeti-Ngorongoro area is largely man-made: over thousands of years it has been moulded by the interaction between the pastoralists, the domestic stock and the wildlife. Extensive herding of domestic stock, grass fires and the grazing of wild ungulates have together created the vast grassland regimes which today hold some of the world's greatest concentrations of wildlife (see Bell, 1971; Jacobs, 1975).

This report has shown that the pastoralists and their herds have had little destructive impact on the Ngorongoro environment over the past twenty years. The rapid human population increase since 1970 was a sequel to the population decrease between 1960 and 1970, and a response to drought conditions in the mid 1970s: people from outside the Conservation Area moved into the grazing reserves of the Ngorongoro highlands. The most recent population estimates indicate that the population level is now falling again. People are returning to the areas from which they came at the onset of the drought. Finally, the increase of the human population in the mid 1970s was not accompanied by a corresponding increase in livestock numbers. Actually the grazing pressure in the Conservation Authority was lower in the late 1970s than in the early 1960s.

Summing up, the relationship between the pastoralists and the Conservation Authority is largely one of conflict and distrust. However, this state of affairs does not reflect an inherent incompatibility between pastoral resource use and environmental conservation; it is rather the result of historical circumstances and a particular type of conservation policy, stressing conservation at the expense of the interests of the local pastoralists. The evidence presented in this report suggests that pastoralism and environmental conservation are compatible in principle. It is a matter of policy and implementation whether they are so also in practice. The final chapter outlines a strategy of development and conservation combining the interests and exigencies of both within the framework of an integral land use policy.

7. Towards an Integrated Approach to Development and Conservation

The findings of the present report have been summarized at the end of each Chapter. Here I want only to restate three major points.

The first has to do with the environmental implications of pastoralism in the Ngorongoro Conservation Area. What was initially believed by the Conservation Authority to be the major problem—that is, the destructive impact of pastoral man on vegetation and wildlife—and which motivated the studies on which this report is based, has in the course of the investigation proved to be a fiction and a problem only insofar as it has directed the course of conservation thinking and action within the Authority. In actual fact the evidence suggests that the current pastoral land use practices present no threat to the environment in Ngorongoro. In a fifty-year perspective, livestock populations have declined rather than grown. The number of people has increased moderately, at least over the past two decades, but since the late 1970s, the trends have reversed: human and small stock populations have decreased, while the cattle population has remained relatively stable. All in all, stocking rates fall well below the estimated carrying capacity of the Conservation Area as a whole. The underlying reason for the long-term environmental stability in the Conservation Area appears twofold: on the one hand, and most importantly, the area has been spared large scale agricultural encroachment and settlement concentrations, and on the other, it is still very marginal with respect to commercial penetration and major infrastructural developments.

The second point to some extent derives from the first. It relates to the apparently falling living standards of the pastoralists. Though they still maintain a standard of living, which in terms of health and nutrition compares well with rural Tanzania as a whole, the Ngorongoro Maasai currently face a deterioration of their food supply situation. This situation is the result of a series of factors and circumstances: a falling ratio of cattle per capita, the recent prohibition on agriculture in the area and the insufficient supplies of grain in the villages. As a consequence, the number of poor pastoralists has increased over the past twenty years and, on the whole, the food standards have fallen. This accounts for the fact that the pastoralists experience a decline in their health situation, and it explains the tremendous concern about cultivation among them. The pastoralists see subsistence cultivation, as a means of supplementing their pastoral economy, as the only solution to the present food shortage.

Studies from other pastoral areas in East Africa show that cultivation in combination with pastoralism rarely is a solution to the economic problems caused by a falling ratio of cattle per capita (cf. Haaland, 1977; Kjaerby, 1979; Jacobs, 1978). On the contrary, pastoralism turned into agro-pastoralism, but not yet integrated into a system of mixed farming, tends in the long run to aggravate the problem: herds are progressively reduced, grazing land reverts to cultivated land, often with soil depletion and erosion on marginal lands as a result. However, the combination of controlled and small scale subsistence cultivation and pastoralism should not be ruled out as a possibility. Combined with efforts to increase the productivity of livestock herds and to regulate the cattle per capita ratio, subsistence cultivation may help the pastoralists to overcome a temporary crisis, the idea being that cultivation itself becomes superfluous over time. In fact, this is the way pastoralists have adapted themselves to temporary food crises in the past and still do in the area north of the Conservation Area. Another possibility would be to promote a long-term development towards a carefully integrated system of mixed farming in selected areas inside or immediately adjacent to the Conservation Area. The whole complex of the inter-relationship between pastoralism, agro-pastoralism and mixed farming, and their environmental implications, deserves more research.

The third point is contingent upon the previous two points, and has to do with the strained relationship between the Conservation Authority and the local pastoralists. This relationship has reached a point of overt antagonism. Both parties interpret the relationship as one of conflicting interests, and there is little mutual understanding and no cooperation between them. This situation has historical roots. It goes back to the eviction of the Siringet and Salei Maasai from the Western Serengeti in 1959, and to the decision in 1961 by the Conservation Authority to exclude the Maasai representatives from the decision-making body of the Authority and the management of the area. Then, in 1975, cultivation was prohibited, and a few years later the pastoralists living in the Ngorongoro Crater were resettled outside the Crater. Enforcement of conservation rules has become increasingly strict. The pastoralists interpret these events as a move on the part of the Conservation Authority away from the original multiple land use policy, towards a single use concept of conservation at the expense of the pastoralists' subsistence rights in the area. Their reaction is resentment, uncooperativeness and occasionally confrontation, albeit still on a minor scale—grass burning, the neglect of certain restrictions on grazing and watering and even retaliatory poaching. All this increases tensions between the pastoralists and the Conservation Authority and tends to be interpreted by the Authority as a major obstacle to the management of the area.

A few more general propositions follow from these conclusions. It has been widely assumed among conservationists and development planners that efforts to develop range water supplies and improve veterinary services in pastoral areas tend to lead to uncontrolled natural herd growth and, hence, overgrazing, trampling and land degradation. Ample evidence has been adduced to show that projects intended to modernize traditional livestock economies in fact increase the destructive environmental impact of pastoralism. The evidence from project areas has been generalized and taken to be valid for pastoral development in general (cf. Talbot, 1972; Prole, 1967).

However, a closer look at the evidence of rapid herd growth and ensuing land degradation proves it to be of limited applicability. Most if not all evidence to this effect turns out to come from the very centres of modernization, from the actual project areas where development efforts have been concentrated. Thus, for example, Talbot—a well-known range ecologist—in discussing environmental consequences of livestock development efforts in Kenya in the 1950s, concludes that "the foci of devastation were the water points, grazing schemes and demonstration ranches" (Talbot, 1972: 704).

In light of the results presented in this report it seems plausible that herd growth around development centres and in project areas is more likely to be due to immigration of people and herds—attracted to the services and facilities in these centres—than to natural herd growth.To take another example from Kenya: the extremely rapid herd growth in Kajiado during the late 1950s, reported by Prole (1967) and attributed by him to an increase in the natural growth rate, seems unrealistic on biological grounds alone (cf. Dahl and Hjort, 1976). Furthermore, the impact of modernization efforts appears often to be exaggerated in the literature; they tend in reality to be more limited in space and time than what is usually believed. In the marginal areas where the majority of the pastoralists live, veterinary services are poor and water development rudimentary. The pastoralists and their herds remain reliant upon traditional resources and management practices, often on shrinking lands and in an increasingly competitive economic and political environment. People and herds may move into project areas and stay there as long as they are able to benefit from services and facilities. But when dams, pipes or pumps break down, when dips are no longer functional, they disperse and move away, much as the Ngorongoro Maasai have moved into and out of the Ngorongoro highlands in response to climatic fluctuations—the succession of rains and droughts.

These conclusions have a direct bearing on the current and future management of the Ngorongoro Conservation Area. Though the relative stability of the pastoral ecosystem in Ngorongoro in part can be related to the fact that Ngorongoro has remained marginal in terms of social and economic development in the conventional sense of commercialization and modernization, it should not be concluded that environmental stability and development are incompatible. It depends upon how conservation and development are conceptualized; it is a question of policy and strategy and the ideas and values underlying them. If development is identified with modernization and industrialization, and if conservation is understood in the narrow sense of wildlife protection at the exclusion of man, then development and conservation are indeed incompatible. But if, on the other hand, development and conservation are understood in the broader sense of sustained land use by man on the basis of environmentally rational forms of resource utilization and the cultural values supporting them, then there is no incompatibility between conservation and development. On the contrary, conservation becomes part and parcel of the development process.

The following is an attempt to outline such an integral strategy of development and conservation, based on the findings of the present report. In all essentials the proposed strategy is in agreement with the recommendations put forth in the new development and management plan for the Ngorongoro Conservation Area submitted to the Conservation Authority in 1982 (see Chapter One, note 2). The overall aim of the strategy is twofold: to improve the living conditions of the pastoralists and to protect the natural heritage of the Ngorongoro Conservation Area. It builds on three fundamental preconditions present in the pastoral community in Ngorongoro: the existing system of pastoral resource use as an adaptive and rational system; the existing social system as an organizational asset; and the indigenous knowledge of the natural environment and its use as an intellectual resource.

This report has shown that the Ngorongoro Maasai practice an environmentally sound and economically rational land use system, evolved in response to the specific resources and constraints of the Ngorongoro environment. Vital to this system is the wide but controlled distribution of domestic stock, the seasonal and rotational use of range resources, the differentiation of the domestic herds in order to spread and reduce the pressure on the resources, and the use of fire as a management tool. These elements are all consistent with and conducive to the overall goals set for the development and management of the Conservation Area. In fact, most range scientists of today tend to agree that extensive pastoralism is the optimal form of utilizing semi-arid and arid rangelands.

Secondly, the social system evolved by the pastoral Maasai—the system of social rules and norms regulating resource use—likewise constitutes an organizational resource of great developmental potential. There exists an elaborate system of rights defining access to specific grazing areas and water sources. Thus, far from being an obstacle to development—as is often implied—the traditional social organization of the Maasai constitutes a fundamental societal asset to be mobilized for development purpose. Thirdly, the social organization of the Maasai and their system of pastoral resource use embody a profound knowledge of the semi-arid savanna environment, a knowledge also manifest in traditional medical and veterinary practices. The richness and potential of the Maasai intellectual legacy is, however, still to be fully revealed by ethno-ecological and ethno-medical research.

The strategy proposed here does not list a number of detailed directives or ready-made solutions "from above". Rather it seeks to formulate a set of fundamental pre-conditions for, and indicate the direction of, a community-based development "from below". In the last instance it is the pastoral community itself that must work out the solutions to its problems. The task of planners and advisers is to help create the pre-conditions for this work and assist in its implementation.

Rights of occupancy

In order to achieve its overall aim, the strategy must first of all seek to secure the home- and subsistence rights of the Ngorongoro Maasai in the Ngorongoro Conservation Area. The pastoralists must know that the land they live in—and live off—cannot be taken from them or used for other purposes without their consent. At present, overriding authority over the land and resources within the Ngorongoro Conservation Area rests with the Conservation Authority. The existing villages in the area lack effective control over village lands. They exist only "on paper", as a potential. Community development, in the direction proposed here, would require a new division of powers between the Conservation Authority, the village governments and the district and regional authorities. Only then could the villages in the Conservation Area attain the status of resource controlling entities in accordance with the Villages and Ujamaa Villages Act of 1975, and as emphasized in the latest (1983) national livestock policy. The current division of the Conservation Area into villages and wards provides a workable framework for attaining this goal, provided that efficient forms of cooperation between villages on the ward level are found.

Participation in decision-making

Secondly, it is necessary that the pastoral villages in the Conservation Area gain full access to the decision-making processes within the Conservation Authority through elected representatives. They must be able to take part in the formulation and implementation of the multiple land use policy which determines their lives. Between 1961 and 1981, the Ngorongoro Maasai entirely lacked representation in the Conservation Authority. Then, in 1981, the Member of Parliament for the Ngorongoro District, who happened to be a Maasai from Ngorongoro, was made a member of the Board of Directors for the Ngorongoro Conservation Area Authority. The goal of full participation in decision-making within the Conservation Authority could be achieved by stipulating that the interests of the resident pastoralists should be permanently represented on the Board of Directors of the Conservation Authority, and by strengthening the section for Community Development within the Conservation Authority. The duties of this section should be to look after the interests of the pastoral villagers and to establish a direct line of communication between the villagers and the Conservation Authority. In cooperation with the village governments the section should be in charge of health and veterinary services, water development and the development of livestock production in general. It should also cooperate closely with the Ecological Research and Monitoring Unit proposed below.

Food supply

A third critical issue which must be addressed by the development strategy is the dry season food shortage. The supply of grain and other essential consumer goods in the villages must be improved, and efforts to increase livestock production must be intensified. Given that crop cultivation is—and most probably will remain—prohibited in the area, grain must be made increasingly available in the local shops. The import and distribution of grain through the Regional Trading Corporation will most likely continue to be insufficient and irregular. The construction of bulk grain stores, one in each ward, where sufficient supplies of grain can be stored, would be a first step towards the improvement of the food supply situation. Village or ward cooperatives, with support from the Conservation Authority, could finance and organize the purchase and transport of grain directly from the agricultural producers. In addition, cooperative grain mills could be set up in connection with each bulk grain store, where grain could be ground into flour on an individual basis when needed. Improvements in the supply and distribution of grain and basic commodities require substantial improvements in transport services. Existing roads have to be upgraded and maintained. This work would require close cooperation with district and regional authorities.

Livestock development

The strategy for livestock development advocated here is based on local resources and geared towards the pastoral producers themselves. It stresses small scale, extensive and mobile livestock production rather than large scale, intensive ranching. Its primary goal is to strengthen the domestically oriented livestock economy; to ensure adequate supplies of milk for consumption rather than promote the production of meat for the market. Higher milk yields is the first development goal, exchange and sale of livestock are secondary goals. An environmentally sound strategy of livestock development along these lines requires a close integration of development efforts in production, pasture management, range water supplies, veterinary services and marketing. The existing villages—as administrative units—may serve as basic units for initiating, implementing and monitoring development efforts. Finally, this type of integrated and community-based development presupposes full local participation and a pragmatically oriented research input.

Range lands and pastures must be protected from any form of alienation or expropriation. Certain conservation rules and restrictions should be reconsidered in the light of the results presented in this report. It is specifically suggested that the complete prohibition on grazing and salt licking in the Ngorongoro, Empakaai and Olmoti Craters should be lifted. Livestock should also be allowed to graze in the Forest Reserve under controlled forms. There is no evidence that grazing in the Craters and in the Forest Reserve has been environmentally detrimental. On the contrary, it has been successfully practiced for generations prior to the current strict conservation regulations. A more flexible implementation of rules and restrictions concerning land use in the Conservation Area would, furthermore, lead to an improved relationship between the pastoralists and the Conservation Authority and hence go a long way in solving the current management problems in the area.

Efforts should be made to lessen the number of wildebeest in areas grazed by domestic stock in order to reduce competition and the risk for disease transmission from wildebeest to domestic stock. The possibility of village based game cropping on a quota basis and of opening up alternative grazing land for wildebeest by systematic and controlled burning should be investigated further (cf. Peterson, 1976). A system whereby villages bordering on National Parks and Game Reserves would be given quotas for game cropping would contribute to the control of poaching and the game population as well as to the improvement of the village meat supply. It would probably also increase the efficiency, and certainly reduce the costs, of game cropping in the Ngorongoro Conservation Area and the Serengeti National Park.[30]

Village sizes and livestock population levels could be controlled by village and ward regulations, defined by the needs of the villagers and the limits set by the carrying capacity of the village lands (including dry and wet season pastures). Similarly, immigration into the Conservation Area could be regulated by the village governments in cooperation with the Conservation Authority. A more even distribution of pastoralists and their herds should be encouraged. At present some areas are under-utilized. This is particularly the case in the Kakesio ward. This area is depopulated principally due to security problems—border hostilities and cattle raiding between the Ngorongoro Maasai and the neighbouring Sukuma people. During the year 1980 alone, the villages of Kakesio and Osinoni lost some 3 000 cattle to Sukuma cattle raiders (Århem, 1981 a: 36; cf. note 25 above). A strengthening of the law enforcement in this zone is therefore necessary to stabilize the livestock economy. The regulations concerning village size, its boundaries and levels of human and animal populations must be derived from a careful assessment of the resource base, the current land use practices, numbers and distribution of people and animals as well as population projections for the near future. Furthermore, the environmental impact of land use practices and development input must be carefully monitored. The Ecological Research and Monitoring Unit of the Conservation Authority (proposed below) in cooperation with the Community Development section should be instrumental in this work.

The water supply situation is, on the whole, not experienced as critical by the pastoralists. However, in certain areas water is scarce, notably in Oldoinyo Oogol, Kakesio, Ilmesigio (part of Olairobi village), Olbalbal and Sendui. In Oldoinyo Oogol, Kakesio, Olbalbal and Sendui the situation is aggravated by the failure of the artificial supplies constructed in the 1940s and 1950s. Therefore, water development efforts must be directed towards the repair and improvement of existing sources (i.e. the boreholes and pumps in Lemuta and Ndjureta, the pipelines in Alaililai-Sendui and Olbalbal). Additional range water supplies (i.e. in Kakesio and Ilmesigio) should be designed as small scale, widely distributed and integrated soil conservation-cum-water harvesting projects based on intermediate technology so that construction, repair and maintenance can be carried out locally (cf. Jacobs, 1978; Kjaerby, 1980).

A principal obstacle to the development of veterinary services is

106

the inadequate supply and distribution of drugs. If drugs were available in the villages people would use them. There exists a very strong motivation to accept and adopt veterinary improvements. At present dipping should not be considered a priority. As long as acaricides are in short supply and dips are operating poorly, dipping may well be a hazard rather than a blessing: irregular dipping in dirty and badly managed dips is likely to be detrimental to livestock health (cf. Jacobs, 1978). Efforts should rather be concentrated on the provision of available drugs to the pastoralists through an improved field service. Specific measures must be taken to control the extensive, illegal sale of veterinary drugs at excessively high prices. Provided that animal populations are kept at acceptable levels within the carrying capacity of the village land, that range water sources are adequate and that the system of rotational grazing is functioning, the dependence on drugs and dipping may be considerably reduced.

There is a low but stable level of commercial offtake from livestock sales in Ngorongoro. Cash incomes from livestock sales appear at least potentially sufficient to meet subsistence needs. The major part of the income derives from sales of livestock outside the official marketing channels. A precondition for the improvement of commercial offtake through official marketing channels is the reinforcement of the marketing system and, above all, the improvement of the supply of grain and other basic commodities in the villages, thus providing greater incentives for livestock sales. At present, the pastoralists see little reason to sell livestock or their produce: there is nothing to buy in the village shops. The current official marketing system with its excessive fees and regulations must be reconsidered in the light of a thorough survey of market performance in pastoral areas. An important factor contributing to poor marketing performance is the cultural barrier between market officials and the pastoral producers: the auctions are performed in Kiswahili and the entire performance at the auction ring is utterly foreign to the pastoralists, underscoring the barrier between the actors and producing a sense of inferiority among the pastoral producers.

There is, finally, a potential for the small scale commercialization of livestock products; the sale of surplus fresh milk could be promoted on a more organized basis, the processing of milk into ghee and cheese is also technically possible by rather simple means, as is the commercial production of hides. All these activities would provide income opportunities for women. Plans to this effect are already under way. The processing and sale of ghee and cheese were of great economic importance among the Ngorongoro Maasai two decades ago (Jacobs, 1978). Thus, the potential for this type of development exists. Another possibility, which would open up alternative sources of income for poor pastoralists, is to involve them in the development of village craft industries directed towards the tourist market.

Health and education

Improvements in community health and education have to start from the conditions given by the pastoral environment and the transhumant mode of life. In light of the fact that, on the one hand, the supply of medical drugs in the villages is—and will remain—inadequate and irregular, and on the other, that the current medical personnel in the area tend to be little motivated and often insufficiently prepared for the task at hand, the development of community health services should concentrate on the dissemination of relevant information in the villages. First priority should be given to the training of local people in basic medicine and hygiene. They have the motivation and cultural competence required for this work. With improved livestock production, food and water supplies, health standards could be expected to rise.

Similarly, the system of basic education has to be adjusted to pastoral conditions and draw on local human resources. Teachers should, as far as possible, be of Maasai origin or at least familiar with their language and culture. This means that efforts should be made to prevail upon formally educated Maasai to do a period of service as school teachers in Maasailand. It should be part of these efforts to involve Maasai women in the teaching scheme. Only Maasai teachers could make the formal education relevant to the pastoral environment and the cultural reality of the Maasai.[31]

Research

It is, finally, recommended that a Research and Monitoring Unit should be established in the Conservation Area. This unit should be staffed with qualified researchers in the fields of biology-ecology (including human ecology and range management) and social sciences, thus covering both the natural and human components of the human-use ecosystem. An important task of the unit should be to investigate and monitor pastoral land use and its environmental impact. Research results should be fed back to the Community Development section and the administrative sections of the Conservation Authority in the form of concrete management proposals and development plans. The unit should ideally cooperate with the Serengeti Research Institute, thus coordinating and complementing the research on the natural ecosystem carried out in the Serengeti National Park with the research on the pastoral ecosystem in the Ngorongoro

Conservation Area. The need for research on extensive rangeland use and ecology is widely recognized nationally and internationally (cf. Saibull, 1980). An ecological research and monitoring unit in the Conservation Area would provide an excellent opportunity for carrying out this type of research and building up a national research competence in this field of vital importance to the development of the livestock sector in Tanzania in general.

As a secondary, but nonetheless important task, the Ecological Research and Monitoring Unit should carry out research on the environmental impact of small scale agriculture and the possibilities of integrating small scale crop cultivation, pastoralism and wildlife conservation in economically and ecologically viable ways. This topic is little explored but of vital importance in land use planning and development at district and regional levels, particularly in northern and central Tanzania. Given the current general tendency for pastoralists to turn into agro-pastoralists and the extremely strongly felt need for subsistence cultivation among the Ngorongoro Maasai, the possibility of controlled small scale agriculture in the Conservation Area as a means of supporting the pastoral economy deserves thorough investigation.

THE WIDER CONTEXT

The strategy of development outlined above implies a local-system approach to development (Galaty, 1981: 20). It starts from local resources, capacities and needs, and sees the local community as the primary beneficiary of development. It places human values above strictly technical ones, thus rejecting a narrow technocratic and growth-oriented approach to development. It represents an orientation towards the quality of life, implying that the goals of development are largely defined by the members of the community themselves. Development becomes in this perspective a way of strengthening the integrity of the community and its self-determining capacities. It aims at the stabilization of resource consumption at a level judged adequate by the people themselves, in accordance with their own cultural standards and values. It presupposes sustainable utilization of the environment and strives towards the retention and maintenance of a maximal variety of natural and man-made environments (cf. Sachs, 1974; Dasmann, 1972).

This notion of development represents a more general approach to development, which challenges the prevailing modernization paradigm with its narrow focus on material growth and its ethnocentric vision of cultural evolution modelled on historic processes in western industrial society. The concepts of "ecodevelopment" and "another development" belong to this increasingly influential counterpoint current in development thinking (Hettne, 1982; Sachs, 1974; Development Dialogue, 1975). They stand—as opposed to the modernization approach—for a culture-oriented and human-centred notion of development and a growing concern for environmental considerations in development planning and practice.

The move away from a narrow and ethnocentric notion of modernization towards a broader concept of development is paralleled by a similar trend in current international conservation thinking. The traditional concept of conservation, which was born out of western, industrial man's devastation of his environment and which implies the separation of man and nature, is giving way to a more inclusive concept of conservation, where man has a place and a role. While the traditional, "insular approach" to conservation—epitomized by the National Park concept—implies resource conservation at the expense of man, this inclusive concept of conservation encompasses both strict biological preservation and sustained land use by man (Dasmann, 1976 a and b; Miller, 1982; Tolba, 1982).

In this perspective conservation becomes an integral part of development. Protected areas are no longer to be the exclusive playgrounds for vacationers, but an inseparable part of human-use ecosystems (McNeely, 1982; Brookfield, 1982). Nature can, in the long run, only be preserved within a system of careful use by man, not as a showcase separated from man. This is the view of development and conservation currently embraced and advocated by the United Nations Food and Agriculture Organization (FAO), the United Nations Environmental Programme (UNEP), the United Nations research and information programme "Man and the Biosphere" (MAB) and the current World Conservation Strategy of the International Union for the Conservation of Nature (approved by the Tanzanian government as the guideline for the national conservation policy).

Underlying the creation of the Ngorongoro Conservation Area and its guiding policy of multiple land use was such an ample and inclusive notion of conservation and development. However, over the past decade, the conservation regime in Ngorongoro has hardened. The insular approach to conservation has increasingly come to dominate the management of the area at the expense of the interests of the indigenous pastoralists. The strategy of development outlined in this report has tried to reconstitute the original intentions of the multiple land use policy. It is the contention of this report that the future of Ngorongoro lies in the careful integration of conservation and development.

110

Appendices

	J	F	M	A	M	J	J	A	S	O	N[a]	D	Total
Tuberculosis	7	3	6	14	8	11	11	15	7	10		10	102
Venereal diseases	20	39	63	37	42	56	40	44	29	35		47	452
Diarrhoea/Dysentery	17	30	87	50	49	86	37	77	49	102		75	659
Malaria	22	32	44	34	13	37	8	87	38	42		44	401
Helminthiasis[b]	18	21	45	48	43	50	38	73	33	45		33	447
Deficiency-related diseases	–	12	34	28	10	22	14	79	16	32		30	277
Eye diseases (Conjunctivitis/Trachoma)	69	45	66	66	42	83	31	150	48	75		80	755
Diseases of the respiratory system	55	80	69	56	67	72	48	113	64	70		92	786
Diseases of the digestive system	6	33	28	15	17	20	27	43	26	25		36	276
Complications during pregnancy/at birth	5	6	5	2	2	2	–	8	6	–		7	43
Skin diseases	17	77	70	76	13	43	15	43	36	39		30	459
Injuries	18	56	41	61	47	58	42	44	36	54		25	482
Others	34	38	75	70	71	88	56	83	68	103		53	739
Total	288	472	633	557	424	628	367	854	456	632		562	5 878

[a] No records available.
[b] Parasitic worms.

	Children[a]		Adults		
	M	F	M	F	Totals
Tuberculosis	29	22	29	22	102
Venereal diseases	12[b]	57[b]	160	223	452
Diarrhoea/Dysentery	282[c]	259[c]	62	56	659
Malaria	116	99	91	95	401
Helminthiasis	202	154	43	48	447
Deficiency-related diseases	81	113	27	56	277
Eye diseases	325[c]	312[c]	57	61	755
Diseases of the respiratory system	243	253	144	146	786
Diseases of the digestive system	89	62	53	72	276
Skin diseases	153	202	54	40	459

[a] Refers to infants and school children (except in the case of venereal diseases).
[b] School children only.
[c] Mostly infants.

Appendix 3. *School Attendance in the Ngorongoro Conservation Area, 1980*

Standard	Average Attendance[a]				
	Boys	%[b]	Girls	%[b]	Totals (100 %)
I	189	65	102	35	291
II	233	66	122	34	355
III	190	66	97	34	287
IV	57	66	29	34	86
V	62	79	16	21	78
VI	48	86	8	14	56
VII	52	91	5	9	57
Totals	831	69	379	31	1 210[c]

[a] The figures refer to average attendance in all schools in the Conservation Area (except that in Nairobi village) during February–August 1980.
[b] Percentage of total attendance at each standard level.
[c] To this figure should be added approximately 144 school children in the primary school of Nairobi village, giving a total of 1 354 for the whole of the Conservation Area. This figure can, in turn, be compared with an estimated school age population (7–13 yrs) of about 3 043 for the year 1978.
Sources: Monthly school reports and census figures from the NCAA.

Appendix 4. *School Attendance in Relationship to Enrollment in the Ngorongoro Conservation Area, 1980*

School	Standard	Enrollment[a]	Attendance[b]
Kakesio	1–7	239	124
Osinoni	1–3	106	67
Esere	1–2	74	19
Endulen	1–7	272	194
Olairobi	1–7	275	178
Mokilal	1–3	144	105
Olbalbal	1–3	93	76
Ilkeepusi	1–3	129	102
Nainokanoka	1–7	216	102
Alaililai	1–3	114	87
Bulati	1–2	81	72
Kapenjiro	1–3	93	74
Totals		1 846	1 100[c]
(%)		(100)	(60)

[a] Number of enrolled children, February 1980.
[b] Average number of children actually attending school during February–August 1980.
[c] The figure does not coincide with the corresponding figure in Appendix 3 because complete information was not available here for all schools in the Conservation Area. The total number of enrolled children in the Conservation Area is estimated at somewhere between 2 000–2 200.

Appendix 5. *Distribution of Basic Services in the Ngorongoro Conservation Area, 1980*

	Kakesio	Osinoni	Esere	Endulen	Olairobi	Olbalbal	Nainokanoka	Alaililai	Nairobi
Health services and schools									
Hospital				1					
Dispensary	1			1			1		
Primary school									
(Standards 1–7)	1			1	1		1		
Universal Primary Education									
(Standards 1–3)		1	1				1	2	1
Livestock related services									
Veterinary centre				1			1		
Dip[a]	(1)		(1)	3	1	1	1	2	
Livestock market[b]				1	(1)		(1)		
Trade and commerce									
Village/Cooperative shop	1			1			1	1	1
Private shop[c]	1		(1)	8	4	2	3		
Bar/Canteen				1	1				
Butchery				1	1				
Transport and communication									
Access road[d]	(+)	−	−	+	+	(+)	+	+	(+)
Bus service					+				
Lorry[e]	+			+					
Administration									
Police station	1			1			1		
CCM Party office				1			1		
NCAA post	1			1		1			

[a] Figures refer to existing dips; parenthesis indicates that the dip is out of order.

[b] Parenthesis indicates that the market is not held regularly.

[c] Parenthesis indicates that the shop is open only periodically.

[d] +accessible all year round; (+) only accessible seasonally or with four-wheel drive vehicle; −no road access.

[e] +indicates the existence of one, or a few, privately owned lorries in the village.

Appendix 6. *Obstacles to Community Welfare: The View of the Pastoralists*

	Kakesio, Osinoni	Esere	Endulen	Olairobi	Olbalbal	Nainokanoka	Alalilai	Nairobi
1. Food shortage	1	1	1	3	1	3	3	1
2. Legal restrictions on land use			2	2	5	1	4	2
3. Water scarcity	4			1	2		1	
4. Poor communications	2					2		4
5. Livestock disease and poor veterinary services		3		5	3			3
6. Poor health services		2		4	4			5
7. Theft of stock		3	4					
8. Poor livestock marketing services							2	

Obstacles to community welfare are listed in order of magnitude as perceived by the villagers (own survey 1980).

Notes

1. It is listed among the first 57 entries on the world Heritage List (Unesco Courier, August 1980).
2. The plan was prepared by a drafting committee consisting of A. Mascarenhas (chairman), K. Århem, H. Fosbrooke, A. Rodgers, L. ole Parkipuny and J. ole Kuwai. The work was partly funded by the World Heritage Fund of UNESCO. At the time of writing (August 1984) the plan has not yet been approved by the Ngorongoro Conservation Area Authority, nor has it, for this reason, been made public.
3. The official figure for the national cattle herd in 1983 was 12.5 million animals (Ministry of Livestock Development, June 1983). It is estimated that the small stock herd is somewhat smaller (Raikes, 1981). Recent official livestock figures are critically examined in Raikes (1981).
4. Jacobs (1975: 406) estimated that there were more than 226 000 pastoral Maasai in Kenya and Tanzania in 1975. Of these, about 62 000 lived in Tanzania. His estimates were based on the 1958 Tanganyikan census and the 1969 Kenya census, adapted and brought up to date by assuming a 2% annual population increase. According to the 1967 national census there were 79 649 Maa-speakers in Tanzania. In 1978, when the latest national census was taken, the total population of Tanzania was 17.5 million.
5. Some 90% of all cattle in East Africa are thought to have died as a result of the rinderpest (Raikes, 1981: 19). See also Kjekshus (1979: 126–32).
6. The information on land alienation in Tanzanian Maasailand in this and the following paragraphs is mainly taken from Hoben (1976), Jacobs (1973), Parkipuny (1975, 1983) and Fosbrooke (pers. comm.).
7. My account of the Masai Range Project is based on Hoben (1976) and Parkipuny (1979).
8. "Operation Imparnati" in Tanzanian Maasailand has been briefly described by Hoben (1976), Ndagala (1982) and Parkipuny (1979).
9. Maasai reactions to villagization are summarized in Hoben (1976) and Ndagala (1982).
10. The ujamaa policy was spelled out in a series of Presidential Papers: "Socialism and Rural Development" (1967), "Freedom and Development" (1968) and "The Development of Ujamaa Villages" (1969).
11. There exist many critical reviews of the ujamaa experiment; see, for example, Hyden (1980) and Boesen (1979).
12. Colonial and post-colonial livestock development policies are described in detail by Raikes (1981).
13. This chapter draws extensively on Dirschl (1966), Fosbrooke (1962, 1972), Parkipuny (1981, 1983) and Saibull (1978).
14. In the Oldoinyo Oogol hills in the northern part of the Conservation Area the land use and settlement patterns deviate from the typical pattern described in this report. Here people and livestock are concentrated in permanent, large settlements in the hills during the wet season and disperse in smaller temporary camps near scarce but reliable water sources on the plains in the dry season. The reason for this reversal of the general pattern is the presence of large herds of wildebeest on the plains in this part of the Conservation Area during the rains.

116

15. The representativity, validity and reliability of the figures are discussed in Århem (1981 a: 20–23). I am currently engaged in a thorough reexamination of all census figures—human as well as livestock—for the Ngorongoro Conservation Area, including the 1980 livestock and settlement count. Some of the figures used in this report may thus be subject to alterations in later publications. I am convinced, however, that the figures, as they stand, are fairly representative of the general population trends in the Conservation Area over the past two decades.

16. The structure of the pastoral population in Ngorongoro shows some significant distortions in the age-distribution of females. This may be due to a combination of under-reporting and over-statement of age for girls in the 10–14 age-group (Århem, 1981 a: 24; cf. Kurji, 1981 a). The general fertility rate (GFR) for the pastoral population in the Conservation Area (1978) is estimated to 128.4 per year. This value is considerably lower than that for the agricultural populations in neighbouring rural districts (Kurji, 1981 a: 19). Fosbrooke (1962) has devised a rough yardstick for comparing natural population increase in populations for which only scant demographic data are available. This device consists of computing the ratio of adult women to the total number of children (under 15) in the population. The 1957 census for the Conservation Area gave a ratio of 159 children per 100 adult women. Fosbrooke concluded that there was a steady but slow natural increase in the pastoral population of Ngorongoro. If the exercise is repeated on the 1978 census data, the ratio turns out 150: 100. It means that the general structure of the pastoral population in Ngorongoro has remained remarkably stable over the past two decades.

17. The study settlements were located in three different ecological zones: Sendui in the eastern highlands, Nasera on the northern plain and Ilmesigio in the intermediate zone between the central highlands and the western plain. Each dry season settlement was studied for a period of 10–12 days, and in each of the settlements three to four households were selected for a detailed study of food intake. The total sample comprised 10 households and 26 meal days. For a fuller description of site selection and research methods, see Århem (1981 b).

18. Food requirements were set at 2 800 Cal/day and 34 g of reference protein/day for the Pastoral Reference Man (PRM), and at 2 600 Cal/day and 27 g reference protein/day for the Pastoral Reference Woman (PRW). The figures are based on Little (1980) and my own observations (Århem 1981 b). The PRM corresponds to 1.0 AE. The PRW accordingly receives the value 0.9 AEs (ibid: 30).

19. The difference in prices between cooperative and private shops is illustrated by the following figures from a few villages (average prices in TShs/kg from Endulen, Kakesio and Nainokanoka) in August 1980: maize flour cost about 2.50 Shs in the village shops and between 3–4 Shs in the private shops; rice 6 Shs in the village shops and 7 in the private shops; sugar 7.50 in the village shops and about 9 in the private shops. In 1982, maize flour was sold in Ngorongoro at about 6 Shs/kg. In June 1984, it was sold by private traders at 30 Shs/kg in the outlying villages and in Karatu at 300 Shs per debe (20 kg). The price varies with season and availability.

20. Since this was written in 1982, even the Endulen-Kakesio road has deteriorated badly. In June 1984 it was in extremely poor shape and is hardly passable during the rains. It has not been maintained since 1978. This is particularly unfortunate, since Endulen has the only hospital in the Conservation Area. The poor condition of the village roads in Ngorongoro stands in sharp contrast to the excellent condition of the "tourist" road from Arusha-Manyara over the Ngorongoro Tourist Headquarters to Seronera in the Serengeti National Park.

21. During a field visit to Ngorongoro in the summer 1984 I was told that the unofficial price of livestock had more than doubled since 1982: a good steer now brought 4–5 000 TShs and a goat between 300–500 TShs.

22. Comparative figures from Kiteto and Monduli districts show an average commercial offtake for the period 1975–78 of 0.5% in Monduli and 2.1% in Kiteto (Terminal Evaluation, 1979).

23. The marketing system in the Arusha Region—particularly the livestock markets in pastoral areas—are examined in detail in Kjaerby (1979). See also Raikes (1981) for a more general discussion.

24. In a study of calf mortality in Oldoinyo Oogol, Ilmesigio and Sendui over a two-year period (1981–83), the highland localities (Ilmesigio and Sendui) showed higher figures (0.279 and 0.276 respectively) than the lowland locality (Oldoinyo Oogol; 0.231) (Homewood and Rodgers, 1984).

25. Cattle raiding has escalated during the past few years in the Kakesio–Endulen area. The Kakesio village borders on Sukumaland, and the Maasai and the Sukuma, being old "enemies", are both involved in the raiding. The availability of rifles and the high "black market" prices for cattle in Tanzania and Kenya may both be partly responsible for the escalation of cattle raiding (cf. Århem, 1981 a: 35).

26. A similar situation has been documented in the USAID-funded Masai Range Project. Dipping frequencies dropped from very high figures at the beginning of the project period to very low figures at the end of the period because of the inadequate supplies of acaricides and the poor operation of the dips (Terminal Evaluation, 1979).

27. The health and food situation among the Ngorongoro Maasai today appears remarkably similar to the situation in Maasailand in general 30 years ago. In his annual medical report for 1951, the District Medical Officer in the Masai District, Dr Hall, writes that Maasailand is one of the most healthy districts in Tanganyika. Malnutrition is not seen in normal years. The staple diet of the Maasai, he reports, is milk and maize meal supplemented by meat. In areas where small stock is plentiful meat forms a large part of the diet. Blood letting from cattle is hardly practiced. The most common diseases are trachoma, gonorrhaea (approximately 60% of the adult population), anthrax (endemic), bronchitis, malaria and syphilis (approximately 30% of the adult population). There is no bilharzia or enteric fever, and dysentery is rare. Tapeworm is about universal, while roundworm is rare (Masai District Book, 1951).

28. In 1984 there was an Austrian doctor at the hospital. Once or twice a month the airborne medical doctor at Wasso in the Loliondo Division visits Endulen hospital.

29. It should perhaps be noted that this solution is not embraced by all conservation officials; there are those who, in their work, try to strike a balance between the needs of the pastoralists and the exigencies of the conservation legislation. But their possibilities to influence policies and decision-making are severely constrained by the current administrative structure in Ngorongoro.

30. Such a system has been proposed and publicized in Tanzania by Dr Alan Rodgers, Dept. of Zoology at the University of Dar er Salaam.

31. The system of boarding schools functioning in Maasailand at the end of the colonial period (the so-called "mother-and-cow" schools) could perhaps serve as a model for a school designed for nomadic or semi-nomadic pastoralists. Apparently this system (as described to me by Maasai informants) was fairly successful and approved by the Maasai themselves. It was discontinued as a result of the restructuring of the national educational system after Independence. The essential features of the system were briefly (a) that children from the same settlement were accompanied by a senior kinswoman, whose responsibility it was to take care of the group of children from the settlement, to provide them with milk and other customary foods, and (b) that each settlement sending children to the school provided some animals as a contribution to the school herd of livestock which would supply the milk for the school children. Furthermore (c) the school boys

were in charge of tending the herd on a rotational basis, while the adult women and girls were in charge of the milking and food preparation. In this way the children could develop their herding skills and keep in touch with the pastoral household duties to which many of them would return after completing school. All in all, this system implied that school children were not totally alienated from their pastoral and family environment while at school; in fact, they brought part of it with them to school. No less important was that they were able to combine, in a relevant way, both theoretical studies and practical experience. Adapted to present circumstances this system would provide an excellent opportunity for teaching improved livestock production techniques and veterinary skills.

References

Århem, K. 1981 *a*, Maasai Pastoralism in the Ngorongoro Conservation Area: Sociological and Ecological Issues. *BRALUP Research Paper* No. 69, Univ. of Dar es Salaam.

Århem, K., in collaboration with Homewood, K. M. and Rodgers, A. 1981 *b*, A Pastoral Food System: The Ngorongoro Maasai in Tanzania. *BRALUP Research Paper* No. 70, Univ. of Dar es Salaam.

Århem, K. 1981 *c*, The Pastoral Population in the Ngorongoro Conservation Area: A Survey of Socio-Economic Conditions. *Background Paper for a New Management Plan in Ngorongoro (mimeo)*. BRALUP, Univ. of Dar es Salaam.

Århem, K. 1982, Är traditionell boskapsskötsel ett hot mot miljön i östafrika? *Ymer*, Årgång 102, Svenska Sällskapet för Geografi och Antropologi, Stockholm.

Århem, K. 1984 *a*, Cultural Identity and the Right to Food: The Case of the Maasai in Tanzania. In A. Eide et al. (eds), *Food as a Human Right*. United Nations University, Tokyo.

Århem, K. 1984 *b*, Another Side of Development: Maasai Pastoralism and Wildlife Conservation in Ngorongoro, Tanzania. *Ethnos*, Vol. 49, III–IV.

Babu, D. S. 1981, *The Serengeti Ecosystem*. Serengeti National Park Booklet.

Baumann, O. 1894, *Durch Massailand zur Nilquelle*. Berlin.

Bell, R. H. V. 1971, A Grazing Ecosystem in the Serengeti. *Scientific American*, 224 (1).

Berreman, G. D. 1979, Himachal: Science, People and 'Progress'. *IWGIA Document* No. 36, Copenhagen.

Berntsen, J. L. 1970, Economic Variation among Maa-speaking Peoples. In B. A. Ogot (ed.), *Ecology and History in East Africa*. Kenya Literature Bureau, Nairobi.

Boesen, J. 1979, Tanzania: From Ujamaa to Villagization. In B. U. Mwansasu and C. Pratt (eds), *Towards Socialism in Tanzania*. Tanzanian Publishing House, Dar er Salaam.

Branagan, D. 1974, A Conflict between Tourist Interests and Pastoralism in the Ngorongoro Highlands of Tanzania. In: *Tourism in Africa and the Management of Related Resources: Proceedings of a Seminar at the Centre of African Studies*, Univ. of Edinburgh, 3rd & 4th of May 1974.

Brandström, P., Hultin, J. and Lindström, J. 1979, Aspects of Agropastoralism in East Africa. *Research Report* No. 51, The Scandinavian Institute of African Studies, Uppsala.

Brookfield, H. 1982, On Man and Ecosystems. *International Social Science Journal* No. 93.

Coe, M. J., Cumming, D. H. and Phillipson, J. 1976, Biomass and Production of Large African Herbivores in Relation to Rainfall and Primary Production. *Oecologia*, 22: 341–354.

Dahl, G. and Hjort, A. 1976, *Having Herds: Pastoral Herd Growth and Household Economy*. Stockholm Studies in Social Anthropology 2. Stockholm.

Dasmann, R. F. 1972, *Planet in Peril: Man and the Biosphere Today*. Penguin Books/ UNESCO.

Dasmann, R. F. 1976 *a*, Toward a Dynamic Balance of Man and Nature. *The Ecologist*, Vol. 6, No. 1.

Dasmann, R. F. 1976 *b*, Natural Parks, Nature Conservation and Future 'Primitive'. *The Ecologist*, Vol. 6, No. 5.

Dirschl, H. J. 1966, Management and Development Plan of the Ngorongoro Conservation Area (mimeo).

Dyson-Hudson, N. 1980, Strategies of Resource Exploitation among East African Savanna Pastoralists. In D. R. Harris (ed.), *Human Ecology in Savannah Environments*. Academic Press N.Y.

Ecosystem Report 1980, *The Status and Utilisation of Wildlife in Arusha Region, Tanzania*. Ecosystems Ltd. Nairobi.

Food and Environment: Reconciling the Demands of Agriculture with Global Conservation. FAO Pamphlet (n.d.).

Fosbrooke, H. A. 1948, An Administrative Survey of the Maasai Social System. *Tanganyika Notes and Records*, No. 26, Dar er Salaam.

Fosbrooke, H. A. 1962, Ngorongoro Conservation Area Management Plan (mimeo).

Fosbrooke, H. A. 1972, *Ngorongoro—The Eighth Wonder*. André Deutsch, London.

Fosbrooke, H. A. 1975, Ngorongoro Conservation Area: 1961–1971 Developments. *Tanzania Notes and Records*, No. 76, Dar es Salaam.

Galaty, J. G. 1981, Land and Livestock among Kenyan Maasai: Symbolic Perspectives on Pastoral Exchange, Change and Inequality. *Journal of Asian and African Studies*, XVI, 1–2.

Galaty, J. G. 1982, Being Maasai; Being "People of Cattle": Ethnic Shifters in East Africa. *American Ethnologist*, Vol. 9, No. 1.

Galaty, J. G. and Aronson, D. R. 1981, Priorities and Pastoralist Development: What is to be done? In Galaty, Aronson, Salzman and Chouinard (eds), *The Future of Pastoral Peoples*. International Development Research Centre, Ottawa.

Glover, P. E. and Gwynne, M. D. 1961, The Destruction of Maasailand. *New Scientist* No. 249.

Grant, H. St. J. 1957, *A Report on Human Habitation in the Serengeti National Park*. Govt. Printer, Dar er Salaam.

Grzimek, B. and Grzimek, M. 1960, *Serengeti Shall Not Die*. Ballantine Books Inc.

Haaland, G. 1977, Pastoral Systems of Production: The Socio-Cultural Context and Some Economic and Ecological Implications. In P. O'Keefe and B. Wisner (eds), *Land Use and Development*. African Environment Special Report 5, London.

Herskovitz, M. J. 1926, The Cattle Complex in East Africa. *American Anthropologist*, 28: 220–72, 361–88, 494–528 and 633–64.

Hettne, B. 1982, Development Theory and the Third World. *SAREC Report* No. 2, 1982 Stockholm.

Hoben, A. 1976, *Social Soundness of the Masai Livestock and Range Management Project*. The USAID Mission in Tanzania, October 1976.

Homewood, K. M. and Rodgers, A. 1984, Pastoralist Ecology in Ngorongoro Conservation Area, Tanzania. *Pastoral Development Network Paper* 17d, Overseas Development Institute.

Huntingford, G. W. 1953, *The Southern Nilo-Hamites, East-Central Africa. Ethnographic Survey of Africa*, Part VIII. London.

Hydén, G. 1980, *Beyond Ujamaa in Tanzania. Underdevelopment and an Uncaptured Peasantry*. Univ. of California Press, Berkeley and Los Angeles.

Iliffe, J. 1979, *A Modern History of Tanganyika*. Cambridge Univ. Press, Cambridge.

Jacobs, A. H. 1973, *Land and Contemporary Politics among the Pastoral Maasai of East Africa*. Paper presented at the American Anthropological Association Symposium on Local Level Change in Contemporary East Africa, New Orleans, November 29, 1973.

Jacobs, A. H. 1975, Maasai Pastoralism in Historical Perspective. In T. Monod (ed.) *Pastoralism in Tropical Africa*. Oxford Univ. Press, London.

121

Jacobs, A. H. 1978, *Development in Tanzanian Maasailand: The Perspective over 20 years: 1957–77*. USAID Report, Tanzania.

Jewell, P. A. 1980, Ecology and Management of Game Animals and Domestic Livestock in African Savannas. In D. R. Harris (ed.), *Human Ecology in Savannah Environments*. Academic Press, N.Y.

Kikula, I. 1983, Woodland and Forest Areal Change in The Ngorongoro Conservation Area. In A. Mascarenhas (ed.), *Ngorongoro: Background Papers for a New Management Plan*. Institute of Resource Assessment Research Paper No 2, Univ. of Dar es Salaam.

King, R. B. 1983, Landform and Erosion in the Ngorongoro Conservation Area. In A. Mascarenhas (ed.), *Ngorongoro: Background Papers for a New Management Plan*. Institute of Resource Assessment Research Paper No. 2, Univ. of Dar es Salaam.

Kjaerby, F. 1979, The Development of Agropastoralism among the Barabaig in Hanang District. *BRALUP Research Paper* No. 56, Univ. of Dar er Salaam.

Kjaerby, F. 1980, The Problem of Livestock Development and Villagization among the Barabaig in Hanang District. *BRALUP Research Report* No. 40, New Series, Univ. of Dar es Salaam.

Kjekshus, H. 1979, *Ecology Control and Economic Development in East African History. The Case of Tanganyika 1850–1950*. Heineman, London.

Kurji, F. 1981 a, Human Population Trends Within and Around the Ngorongoro Conservation Area: The Demographic Settings. *BRALUP Research Report* No. 44, New Series, Univ. of Dar es Salaam.

Kurji, F. 1981 b, Wildlife Ecology: A Bibliography of Some Studies in Tanzania. *BRALUP Research Report* No. 46, New Series, Univ. of Dar es Salaam.

Kuwai, J. L. 1981 a, Livestock Development in the Ngorongoro Conservation Area (mimeo).

Kuwai, J. L. 1981 b, Reasons for a New Development and Management Plan for the Ngorongoro Conservation Area (typewritten manuscript).

Little, M. 1980, Designs for Human-Biological Research among Savanna Pastoralists. In D. R. Harris (ed.), *Human Ecology in Savannah Environments*. Academic Press, N.Y.

Makacha, S. 1980, Rainfall Distribution in the Ngorongoro Conservation Area. *NCAA Report* 10.

Mascarenhas, A. 1979, An Application from the Ngorongoro Conservation Area Authority (Tanzania) to the World Heritage Fund. BRALUP, Univ. of Dar es Salaam.

Mascarenhas, A. 1983, Ngorongoro: A Challenge to Conservation and Development. *Ambio*, Vol. 12, No. 3–4.

McNeely, J. A. 1982, Protected Areas Have Come of Age. *Ambio*, Vol. XI, No. 5.

Merker, M. 1910, *Die Masai. Etnographische Monographie eines ostafrikanischen Semitenvolkes*. Berlin.

Miller, K. 1982, Parks and Protected Areas: Considerations for the Future. *Ambio*, Vol XI, No. 5.

Ministry of Livestock Development, 1983. The Livestock Policy of Tanzania. The United Republic of Tanzania, June 1983.

Ndagala, D. K. 1982, "Operation Imparnati": The Sedentarization of the Pastoral Maasai in Tanzania. *Nomadic Peoples*, No. 10.

Parkipuny, L. M. S. 1975, *Maasai Predicament Beyond Pastoralism*. Unpublished M. A. Dissertation, Inst. of Development Studies, Univ. of Dar es Salaam.

Parkipuny, L. M. S. 1979, Some Crucial Aspects of the Maasai Predicament. In A. Coulson (ed.), *African Socialism in Practice: The Tanzanian Experience*. Spokesman, Nottingham.

Parkipuny, L. M. S. 1981, On Behalf of the People of Ngorongoro: A Discussion of the Question, Does the Future of Ngorongoro Lie in Livestock vs Wildlife or Livestock and Wildlife. *Background Paper for a New Management Plan in Ngorongoro (mimeo). BRALUP,* Univ. of Dar es Salaam.

Parkipuny, L. M. S. 1983, *Maasai struggle for home rights in the land of the Ngorongoro Crater.* Paper read at the XI International Congress of Anthropological and Ethnological Sciences, Vancouver, August 20–25.

Pearsall, W. H. 1957, Report on an Ecological Survey of the Serengeti National Park, Tanganyika. *Oryx* 4: 71–136.

Peterson, D. D. 1976, A Survey of Livestock and Wildlife Seasonal Distribution in Areas of Maasailand adjacent to the Tarangire National Park (mimeo). USAID, Masai Livestock and Range Management Project.

Peterson, D. D. and Peterson, T. 1980, Range Management in Arusha Region. Discussion Paper for the Arusha Planning and Village Development Project.

Prole, J. H. B. 1967, Pastoral land use. In W. T. W. Morgan (ed.), *Nairobi: City and Region.* Oxford Univ. Press.

Raikes, P. L. 1981, *Livestock Development and Policy in East Africa.* Publications from the Centre for Development Research 6, Copenhagen. Scandinavian Institute of African Studies, Uppsala.

Sachs, I. 1974, Ecodevelopment. *Ceres,* Nov.–Dec. 1974.

Saibull, S. A. 1968, Ngorongoro Conservation Area: A Case Study in Elements of Lands Use. *East African Agricultural and Forestry Journal,* Special Issue, Vol. 33.

Saibull, S. A. 1978, The Policy Process: The Case of Conservation in the Ngorongoro Crater Highlands. *Tanzania Notes and Records,* No. 83, Dar es Salaam.

Saibull, S. A. 1980, *Cattle-Keeping Policy and Practice in Tanzania.* Paper presented at the 7th Scientific Conference of the Tanzania Society of Animal Production, 27–30 May, 1980.

Saitoti, Ole T. and Beckwith, C. 1980, *Maasai.* Harry N. Abrahams Inc., Publishers, N.Y.

Sankan, S. S. 1971 (1980), *The Maasai.* Kenya Literature Bureau, Nairobi.

Sinclair, A. R. E. 1979, The Eruption of the Ruminants. In A. R. E. Sinclair and M. Norton-Griffiths (eds), *Serengeti: Dynamics of an Ecosystem.* The Univ. of Chicago Press, Chicago and London.

Ståhl, M. 1980, *Tanzania: Landanalys.* SIDA, Stockholm.

Talbot, L. M. 1972, Ecological Consequences of Rangeland Development in Masailand, East Africa. In T. Farvar and J. P. Milton (eds), *The Careless Technology: Ecology and International Development.* Natural History Press, N.Y.

Terminal Evaluation of the Masai Livestock and Range Management Project, Tanzania, USAID Report, 1979.

Tolba, M. K. 1982, *Development without Destruction: Evolving Environmental Perspectives.* Natural Resources and Environment Series, Vol. 12. Tycooly Int. Publ. Ltd, Dublin.

The Unesco Courier, August 1980. The World Heritage List: The First 57 Entries. Paris.

Western, D. 1982, Amboseli National Park: Enlisting Landowners to Conserve Migratory Wildlife. *Ambio,* Vol. XI, No. 5.

What Now? Another Development. *Development Dialogue,* No. 1–2, 1975.

123

Uppsala Research Reports in Cultural Anthropology

1. Kerstin Eidlitz: *Revolutionen i norr* (with English summary). 1979.
2. Bo Gärtze: *Kinesisk wushu.* 1981.
3. Kaj Århem: *Pastoral Man in the Garden of Eden. The Maasai of the Ngorongoro Conservation Area, Tanzania.* 1985.*

* Published within the African Studies Programme, Department of Cultural Anthropology, University of Uppsala.